ENGLISH ESTATES
OF AMERICAN COLONISTS

ENGLISH ESTATES
OF AMERICAN COLONISTS

American Wills and Administrations
in the Prerogative Court of Canterbury,
1610-1699

By Peter Wilson Coldham

Baltimore
GENEALOGICAL PUBLISHING CO., INC.
1980

Published by Genealogical Publishing Co., Inc.
Baltimore, Maryland, 1980
Copyright © 1980
Peter Wilson Coldham
Surrey, England
All Rights Reserved
Library of Congress Card Number 80-68237
International Standard Book Number 0-8063-0905-9
Made in the United States of America

ENGLISH ESTATES OF AMERICAN COLONISTS: 1610-1699

INTRODUCTION

This second volume of abstracts from Prerogative Court of Canterbury (PCC) Probate and Administration Act Books for the period 1610-1699 is intended as a companion work to that already published for 1700-1799. The prefatory notes included in that volume require little expansion and should be read as an introduction.

For the compilation of the present volume entries in the PCC Act Books from 1610 onwards [1] have been examined and abstracts made of those relating to settlers in mainland America and to their families. The resulting material has then been verified and supplemented by comparing it with the principal printed works listing American wills and administrations in the PCC. This has provided the opportunity to include a note of those wills made by Englishmen who named relatives living in the American colonies or who had interests there.

Only one further comment seems necessary: the earlier the Act Books, the more meager the information they give. Amongst the many thousands of Acts recording deaths *in parts overseas* only a miniscule proportion name the actual country or colony.

Printed Sources and Abbreviations Used

The printed collections used to supplement abstracts from the PCC Act Books were:

American Colonists in English Records, Vols. 1 & 2, London, 1932 and 1933, by George Sherwood. Abbreviated as Sh.

Genealogical Gleanings in England, Vols. 1 & 2, New England Historic Genealogical Society, Boston, 1901, by Henry FitzGilbert Waters. Abbreviated as Wa.

Immigrants to America Appearing in English Records, Everton Publishers, Inc., 1976, by Frank Smith. Abbreviated as Sm.

National Genealogical Society Quarterly, Washington; articles by Peter Wilson Coldham. Abbreviated as NGSQ.

Virginia Gleanings in England, Genealogical Publishing Co., Inc., Baltimore, 1980, by Lothrop Withington. Abbreviated as Wi.

It should be noted, however, that references to printed sources have been included only when those sources provide either a transcript or a substantial abstract of the original will. Notes in the text appearing in parentheses have been taken from sources other than the Act Books.

Peter Wilson Coldham
Purley, Surrey,
England.

Pentecost 1980
AMDG.

Abstracts from documents in Crown copyright are published by permission of Her Britannic Majesty's Stationery Office.

---

[1] *Administration Act Books* (PROB 6), Volumes 7-75. The volume for February 1643 to April 1644 is wanting.

Probate Act Books (PROB 8), Volumes 14-92. The volumes for 1650, 1653, 1654 and 1662 are wanting but the gaps have to some extent been made up by consulting the will registers (PROB 11).

ENGLISH ESTATES
OF AMERICAN COLONISTS

Abbes, Edward, who died in Virginia. Probate to relict Sarah
Abbes. (May 1637). Sh.Wi.

Abbott, John, of St. Saviour, Southwark, Surrey. (Son Josiah
Abbott of New England). Probate to Sampson Eyton and Mary
Eyton. (July 1693). Wa.

Abington, John, of St. Faith the Virgin, London. (Lands in
Maryland). Administration with will to sister Muriel Parney
and niece by a brother Muriel Abington; John Abington re-
nouncing. (July 1694). Revoked and granted to William
Isatt, guardian of John and Charles Nelmes. (Apr. 1698).
Wa.

Achley, John, of London, merchant, who died abroad, bachelor.
(Trader to Virginia). Probate to John Dolman. (Nov. 1666).
New grant August 1667. See article in NGSQ 67/61.

Acrod, Benjamin, of Hackney, Middlesex, who died in Pennsylvania. Administration to relict Sarah Acrod. (July 1684).
Revoked and probate granted to John Acrod after sentence
for validity of will, with similar powers reserved to
Richard White. (Dec. 1684).

Adams, Elizabeth, of Rotherhithe, Surrey, widow. (Son in
Virginia). Probate to daughter Mary Adams. (Dec. 1660).
Wa.

Addams, John, of St. Botolph Aldgate, London, who died in Virginia, bachelor. Administration to mother Anne Addams.
(Aug. 1688).

Aishley - see Ashley.

Alcock, George, of St. Katherine Creechurch, London. (Lands
in New England). Probate to Benjamin Walker and Peter
Thatcher with similar powers reserved to Zachariah Whitman.
(Mar. 1677). Wa.

Alderne, Thomas, of Hackney, Middlesex. (Lands in New England).
Probate to relict Dorothy Alderne with similar powers reserved to Owen Row, Thomas Ludington and John Greene. (June
1657). Revoked on death of relict and administration to
Edward Alderne, doctor of laws, uncle and guardian of the
children Thomas, Owen, Edward and Dorothy Alderne. (Dec.
1660). Wa.

Alleine, Josias, of New England, bachelor. Administration to
brother Jonathan Alleine. (June 1678).

Allen, George, of Queen's Ferry, Scotland, who died at sea near
Virginia, bachelor. Administration to William Leget,
attorney for sisters Isabel, Elizabeth and Merian Allen
alias Orie. (Jan. 1673).

Allen, James, of Kempston, Bedfordshire. (Son Roger Allen in
New England). Probate to son John Allen. (Jan. 1658).
Sh.Wa.

Allen, John, of Holborn, Middlesex, who died in Maryland.
Probate to relict Elizabeth Allen. (Jan. 1675). Revoked
on her death and administration to William Harmer, brother
and administrator to executor Timothy Harmer deceased; other
executor Paul Wheeler having also died. (June 1688). Wi.

Allin, Silvester, of Tower Precinct, London, who died abroad,
(on voyage to Virginia). Probate to relict Elizabeth Allin.
(Mar. 1636). Sh.Wi.

Allen, Thomas, of City of London. (Brother Bozonne in New
England. Probate to brother William Allen. (Feb. 1647).
Sh.Wa.

Allright, William, of Aborfield, Berkshire. (Daughter Margaret Avery in New England). Probate to son William Allright. (May 1667).

Allsopp, John, of Bonsall, Derbyshire. (Brothers and sister in New England). Probate to Roger Jackson with similar powers reserved to Dorothy Hopkinson. (Feb. 1647). Wa.

Alsopp, Rev. Josias, of Combe Nevell, Kingston, Surrey. (Sister Elizabeth Rosseter in New England). Probate to John Bestwood. (Oct. 1666). Wa.

Alsop, Timothy, of St. Mary Somerset, London. (Sister in New England). Administration with will to relict Martha Alsop. (Aug. 1664). Wa.

Allwood, Richard, of New Sarum, Wiltshire. (Brother Edmond Batter in New England). Probate to relict Elizabeth Allwood. (Mar. 1645). Wa.

Altham, Emmanuel, died abroad, bachelor. (Bequest to Mrs. Thomsin in New England). Administration with will to nephew John Altham; brother Sir Edward Altham having died. (Nov. 1638). Sh.

Ambrose, Peter, of Toxteth, Lancashire. (Bequest to Joshua and Daniel Henshawe in New England). Probate to relict Judith Ambrose with similar powers reserved to Nehemiah Ambrose. (Jan. 1653). Wa.

Amias, Francis, of Gosnarch, Lancashire, (adventurer in Virginia). Probate to brother Paul Amias. (July 1622). Wi.

Amsed, James, of Virginia. Administration to principal creditor Rebecca Anyon. (Dec. 1696).

Anderson, David, of Boston, New England. who died at sea. Administration to principal creditor Robert Thomson. (Jan. 1678). Revoked and granted to John Phillipps, attorney for relict Catherine Anderson of Charles Town, New England. Feb. 1678).

Anderson, Henry, of Bantam, East Indies. (Father John Anderson of Boston, New England). Probate to brother David Anderson with similar powers reserved to father John Anderson. (Feb. 1676). Wa.

Anderson, John, of New England. Probate to John Phillips with similar powers reserved to relict Mary Anderson. (Feb. 1678). Wa.

Anderson, William, of Shadwell, Middlesex, who died in Virginia, bachelor. Administration to principal creditor Anne Allen. (Sept. 1680).

Andrewes, John, of Cambridge, merchant. (Son John Andrewes in Virginia). Probate to relict Hester Andrewes. (June 1616). Wi.

Andrewes, John, of Barbados. (Sister Deborah, wife of Robert Fenn of Boston, New England). Administration with will to Samuel Wild during minority of brother Samuel Andrewes and during absence abroad of Morgan Powell and Thomas Sprigg; administration to William Creeke of March 1649 withdrawn. (Feb. 1650). Sh.Wa.

Angell, William, of St. Bartholomew by Exchange, London. (Friend Henry Kersey in Virginia). Probate to relict Anne Angell and Richard Angell. (Feb. 1637). Wi.

Angier, Bezaliel, of Dedham, Essex. (Brother Edmund Angier in New England). Probate to relict Anne Angier. (Nov. 1678). Wa.

Angier, Samuel, of Dordrecht, Holland. (Brother Edmund Angier in New England). Probate to Sir Richard Ford, alderman of London, attorney for relict Barbara Angier during her absence abroad. (May. 1667). Wa.

Anthonye, Charles, of St. John Zachary, London, (adventurer to
    Virginia). Probate to son Thomas Anthonye. (Nov. 1615).
    Revoked on his death and administration to relict Elizabeth
    Anthonye. (Sept. 1623). Sh.Wi.
Anthony, David, of Virginia, bachelor. Administration with will
    to Margaret, wife of executor James Dicks now overseas.
    (July 1676).
Anthony, Francis, doctor of medicine of St. Bartholomew the Great,
    London. (Goods in Virginia). Probate to relict with similar
    powers reserved to Stephen Lo-sure. (June 1623). Wa.
Archbell, John, of ship *Ephraim* who died at Virginia. Probate
    by decree to Hannah, wife of Alexander Tompson with similar
    powers reserved to the said Alexander. (Nov. 1692).
Archer, John, clerk, who died abroad. (Brother in New England).
    Administration with will to relict Susan Archer; no executor
    having been named. (Mar. 1649). Sh.
Archer, Robert, of St. Dunstan in West, London, who died at
    Carolina. Administration to sister Elizabeth Cave, widow;
    relict Mary Archer renouncing. (Dec. 1691).
Archer, Roger, of Virginia. Administration to principal creditor
    John Pennell. (Mar. 1642).
Argall, Sir Samuel, who died overseas. (Lands in Virginia).
    Probate to Richard Hanes with similar powers reserved to
    brother John Argall. (Mar. 1626). Double probate to John
    Argall. (May 1626). Wa.
Argent, George, of Hoxton, Middlesex. (Daughter Anne Ivey in
    Virginia). Probate to cousins John Langley and John Glascock.
    (Apr. 1654). Wi.
Arnold, Edward, of Virginia, widower. Administration to prin-
    cipal creditor Thomas Allen. (May 1672).
Arnold, Richard, citizen and goldsmith of London. (Nephew Thomas
    Arnold in New England). Probate to Thomas Lofty. (Nov. 1644).
    Wa.
Arnold, Thomas, of St. Sepulchre, London, who died at Carolina.
    Administration to sister Elizabeth Arnold; father Jeremiah
    Arnold renouncing. (Nov. 1688).
Arrowsmith, Hugh, of ship *Edgar* who died at sea (and of New York).
    Administration with will to Thomas Anger, attorney for Thomas
    Bishop and John Tongue during their absence abroad; no
    executor having been named. (Sept. 1691).
Arrowsmith, John, of Virginia, bachelor, who died overseas.
    Administration to Dorcas, wife of principal creditor Gerrard
    Dobson now overseas. (July 1688). Revoked and granted to
    Gerard Dobson. (Oct. 1688).
Arthington, Robert, of London, who died abroad, (intending a
    voyage to Virginia). Probate to sister Mary Eldred. (May
    1651). Sh.
Aishley, Edward, of Ratcliffe, Middlesex, who died in Virginia.
    Administration to James Shaw, guardian of only child Eliza-
    beth Aishley during her minority. (Aug. 1656).
Ashley, John, of Virginia. Administration to Christopher Rowe,
    grandfather and guardian of only child Joane Ashley. (May
    1657).
Ashton, James, of Stafford Co., Virginia. Probate to John Foster
    with similar powers reserved to John Ashton. (July 1687).
Astwood, John, of Milford, New England. Probate to son Samuel
    Astwood. (Aug. 1654). Wa.
Atkins, Edward, of Chard, Somerset, who died in Virginia or
    abroad. Administration to son Richard Atkins. (Sept. 1652).
Atkins, John, of Virginia, bachelor. Administration with will
    to brother William Atkins; no executor having been named.
    (Oct. 1624). Revoked on his death and granted to brother

3

Richard Atkins, guardian of children Elizabeth, George,
Anne and Lee Atkins during their minority. (Aug. 1626).
Revoked on the death of Richard Atkins and granted to
brother Humfrey Atkins. (June 1627). Sm.Wi.
Atkins, John the elder, of Chard, Somerset. (Grandchild born
in Virginia). Probate to relict Katherine Atkins. (Nov.
1636). Wi.
Atkins, Mary - see Wade.
Atkins, Richard, of Maryland, bachelor. Administration to
principal creditor Thomas Ellis. (June 1669).
Atkinson, Francis, of H.M.S. *Deptford* who died at Virginia.
Probate to James Bowerman. (Dec. 1695).
Atkinson, William the younger, of St. Vedast, Foster Lane,
London, (intending for Virginia). Probate to father William
Atkinson with similar powers reserved to Thomas and Ralph
Atkinson. (Aug. 1613). Sh.Wi.
Atterbury, Richard, who died abroad, bachelor, (resident in
Virginia). Probate to brother William Atterbury. (June
1638). Wi.
Augur, Margery, of St. Andrew Hubbard, London, widow. (Son
Nicholas Augur in New England). Probate to daughter Hester
Augur. (Oct. 1658). Wa.
Aungier, John, of Drome Derrick, Cavan Co., Ireland, clerk,
who died at St. Clement Danes, Middlesex, (or in Virginia).
Probate to relict Anne Aungier. (Apr. 1692).
Austin, Joseph, of Shadwell, Middlesex, (and late of New
England). Probate to Mary Yems. (Sept. 1679).
Austin, Thomas, of H.M.S. *Richmond* who died at New York.
Probate to Thomas Frampton. (June 1694).
Avery, John, of Dorchester Co., Maryland. Administration with
will to Cuthbert Haslewood, brother of John Haslewood now
overseas, husband of the relict Anne Haslewood alias Avery
now deceased. (Aug. 1683).
Axtell, Daniel, of Stoke Newington, Middlesex, who died at
Carolina. Administration with will to Walter Needham, M.D.,
attorney for relict Rebecca Axtell now in Carolina. (July
1687).
Axtell, Nathaniel, of St. Peter's, St. Albans, Hertfordshire.
(Mentions Thomas Buckingham, Richard Miles and Peter Pridden
in Virginia and New England). Probate to brother Daniel
Axtell. (June 1640). Wi.
Ayres, Thomas, of Carolina, bachelor. Administration to
brother John Ayres. (June 1691).

Babb, Thomas, of Stepney, Middlesex, who died in Virginia.
Administration to relict Eleanor Babb. (July 1646).
Revoked on her death and granted to only child Mary Babb.
(July 1655).
Bache, Thomas, of Over Pen, Staffordshire. (Nephew Peter Buck
in Virginia). Administration with will to daughter Mary
Dyson; no executor having been named. (July 1674). See
NGSQ 62/273.
Bacon, Richard, of Stepney, Middlesex, (bound for Virginia).
Probate to William Chalke. (Dec. 1687).

4

Badnadge, Thomas, of ship *Honor* going to Virginia, who died at
sea. Administration to relict Abigall Badnadge. (June 1659).
Baker, John, of St. Bride's, London. (Sister Jane Gilbert of
New England). Probate to relict Jane Baker. (June 1664).
Wa.
Baker, John, of Stepney, Middlesex, who died in New England.
Probate to relict Sarah Baker. (Oct. 1678).
Baker, Richard, of Stonedeane, Chalfont, Buckinghamshire.
(Lands in Pennsylvania). Probate by solemn affirmation to
Rebecca Baker with similar powers reserved to Winifred
Baker. (Nov. 1697).
Baker, Roger, who died overseas, (of Wapping, Middlesex, with
lands in Maryland). Administration with will to daughter
Mary, wife of Thomas Johnson; executor Abraham Hughes
renouncing. (Jan 1688). Wa.
Baker, Thomas, citizen and apothecary of London. (Brother
Richard Baker in Virginia). Probate to relict Sarah Baker;
son Thomas Baker renouncing. (May 1654). Wi.
Baker, Thomas, of ship *Elizabeth* who died in Virginia. Probate
to sister Mary Bennett alias Baker with similar powers
reserved to John Bennett. (Aug. 1698).
Balfoure, William, of Virginia. Probate to Alexander Blair.
(Sept. 1686).
Ball, James, of Waterton near Boston in parts overseas, bachelor.
Administration to Joane Ball, mother of niece and next of
kin Anne Ball. (Apr. 1672).
Bancks, Richard, of Carolina. Administration to mother Joane
Bancks during absence abroad of relict Mary Bancks. (May
1682).
Banford, Charles, of Boston, New England, who died on H.M.S.
Nonsuch. Administration to Anne Gibbons, wife and attorney
of principal creditor William Gibbons in New England. (Apr.
1695).
Barham, Anne, of Canterbury, Kent, widow. (Kinsman Anthony
Barham in Virginia). Probate to Thomas Lyne. (July 1640).
Wi.
Barham, Anthony, of Mulberry Island, Virginia. Probate to
Edward Major and William Butler. (Sept. 1641). Sh.Wa.
Barker, Thomas, of Stepney, Middlesex, who died in Maryland.
Administration to relict Mary Barker. (Sept. 1698).
Barnabe, Richard, of All Hallows, Lombard Street, London.
(Brother John Barnabe in Virginia). Administration with will
to sister Elizabeth, wife of George Rookes, during minority
of children Elizabeth and Mary Barnabe. (July 1636). Wi.
Barnes, Thomas, of H.M.S. *Rose* who died near New England.
Administration with will to Susan Harbison, daughter of
relict Elizabeth Barnes alias Harbison, who died before
administering. (Nov. 1690).
Barrett, Robert, of Christ Church, Surrey, who died in Virginia.
Administration to relict Sarah Barrett. (Nov. 1698).
Bartlett, George, of St. Mary Somerset, London. (Daughter-in-
law Elizabeth Westcoate in Virginia). Probate to Elizabeth
Ambler, widow. (Mar. 1660). Wi.
Barton, William, of H.M.S. *Play's* prize. (Children in Penn-
sylvania). Administration with will to John Bunce, attorney
for Matthew Butts and Robert Walker now at sea or abroad;
no executor having been named. (Oct. 1697).
Baskerville, Henry, citizen and fishmonger of London. (Brother
John Baskerville in Virginia). Probate to brother Lawrence
Baskerville. (May 1676). Wi.
Bate, Richard, of Lydd, Kent. (Mother Alice Bate in New England).
Probate to son James Bate. (Apr. 1657). Sh.Wa.

Bawdon, Sir John, of All Hallows the Great, London. (Lands in
New England). Probate to relict Dame Letitia Bawdon. (Jan.
1689). New grant November 1720. Sh.
Baynton, John, of Bristol, (bound for Virginia). Administra-
tion with will to Charles Harford and William Bathe, guar-
dians of son Benjamin Baynton. (Jan. 1690). Wi.
Baytop, Thomas the elder, of Virginia, widower. Administration
to Daniel Baytop, guardian of only child Thomas Baytop.
(Jan. 1692). Revoked and granted to said Thomas Baytop on
his coming of age. (Sept. 1699).
Beale, Christopher, of East Furleigh, Kent. (Daughter Margaret
in New England). Probate to relict. (June 1651). Wa.
Beard, William, of Virginia. Probate to Alexander Chill.
(Oct. 1646). Sh.Wi.
Beauchamp, Abel, of Worcester who died at Virginia, bachelor.
Administration to brother Richard Beauchamp. (Dec. 1678).
Beauchamp, John, of St. Giles Cripplegate, London. (Lands in
Virginia). Probate to uncle James Jauncy and brother William
Beauchamp. (Sept. 1668). Wi.
Beavay, Thomas, of Bristol. (Son Thomas Beavay in Virginia).
Probate to relict Mary Beavay. (Apr. 1657). Wa.
Becon, John, of Ratcliffe, Stepney, Middlesex, who died in
Virginia. Administration to principal creditor Giles Shute;
relict Mary Becon renouncing. (June 1678).
Beheathland, John, of St. Endellion, Cornwall, who died abroad,
(bound for Virginia), bachelor. Administration with will to
Charles Beheathland; no executor having been named. (Oct.
1639). Sh.Sm.Wi.
Bell, Robert, of Deptford, Kent. (Cousin Anne Bickley in Vir-
ginia). Probate to Richard Chapman. (Feb. 1657). Wi.
Bell, Susan, of All Hallows Barking, London, widow. (Bequest
to Anne, wife of John Elliott of New England). Probate to
son Thomas Bell. (Mar. 1673). Wa.
Bell, Thomas the elder, of All Hallows Barking, London. (Nephew
Thomas Makins in New England). Probate to relict Susan Bell.
(May 1672). Wa.
Benbowe, Thomas, of ship *St. Andrew*. Administration to Joanna
wife of principal creditor Roger Frost in Virginia; relict
Catherine Benbowe renouncing. (Jan. 1673).
Bennett, John, of St. Gabriel, Fenchurch Street, London. (Lands
in Maryland). Probate to Margery Jones. (May 1698).
Benet, Richard, of St. Bartholomew by Exchange, London, who
died in Virginia. Administration to brother Edward Benet;
relict Judith Benet renouncing. (June 1627).
Bennett, Richard, who died overseas, (in Virginia). Probate to
James Joffey with similar powers reserved to Thomas Hodges,
Edmund Belson and Robert Peelle. (Aug. 1676). Wa.
Bennington, Richard, who died overseas, (bound to Virginia).
Probate to Robert Arnold. (Feb. 1612). Sh.
Benskin, Francis, of St. Martin in Fields, Middlesex. (Son
Henry Benskin of Virginia). Probate to children Thomas and
Frances Benskin. (Jan 1692). Wa.
Benskin, Henry, formerly of St. Martin in Fields, Middlesex,
but late of Virginia. Probate to Alexander Roberts and
Thomas Whitfield. (Oct. 1692). Wa.
Berkeley, Sir William, Governor of Virginia, who died at
Twickenham, Middlesex. Administration to Alexander Cul-
peper, brother of relict Lady Frances Berkeley during her
absence. (July 1677).
Best, Nicholas, of Stratford by Bow, Middlesex, who died in
Maryland, widower. Administration to daughter Rebecca,
wife of Aaron Hawkins. (Sept. 1686).

Beton, John, of Ratcliffe, Stepney, Middlesex, who died at
    Virginia. Administration to principal creditor Giles Shute;
    relict Mary Beton renouncing. (June 1678).
Bettris, Edward, of Oxford, surgeon. (Lands in Pennsylvania).
    Probate to relict Anne Bettris. (Feb. 1685). Wa.
Bew, Rigoult, of Virginia who died at St. Giles Cripplegate,
    London, bachelor. Limited administration to Micajah Perry
    of London, merchant, attorney for sister Mary Thurston,
    Elizabeth Iremonger and Sarah Dawson. (Sept. 1697).
    Revoked on production of will and probate granted to Samuel
    Dawson with similar powers reserved to Elizabeth Ironmonger
    and Robert Thurston. (July 1698).
Bigge, John, of Whitechapel, Middlesex. (Bequest to Frances
    Rogers of Virginia, spinster). Probate to relict Joan Bigg.
    (Sept. 1636). Wa.
Bigg, John, of Maidstone, Kent. (Mother, brother and sister in
    New England). Probate to Andrew Broughton. (Feb. 1643). Wa.
Biggs, Richard, of West Sherley Hundred, Virginia. Administration
    with will to relict Sarah Biggs; no executor having been named.
    (Aug. 1626). Sh.Sm.Wi.
Binding, Sarah, of Chertsey, Surrey, widow. (Daughter Sarah,
    wife of Richard Buckley of Boston, New England). Probate
    to Jeremiah Dyke and Abigail Dyke. (Sept. 1687). Wa.
Bird, John, of St. Sepulchre, London, who died in Virginia.
    Administration to Robert Bernard. (Feb. 1674).
Birt, Thomas, of Hershey, Gloucestershire, who died at Boston,
    New England, bachelor. Administration to brother Giles Birt.
    (Oct. 1670).
Blackler, Joas, of Tower of London, who died at Virginia, bache-
    lor. Administration to brother John Blackler. (Jan. 1699).
Blackmore, Arthur, of St. Gregory, London. (Daughter Susan,
    wife of William Corker of Virginia). Probate to relict
    Elizabeth Blackmore. (Mar. 1664). See NGSQ 67/215.
Blagge, Edward, of Plymouth, Devon, who died at Virginia.
    Administration to relict Patience Blagge. (Mar. 1693).
Blagrave, Edward, of St. Margaret, Westminster, Middlesex, who
    died at Virginia, bachelor. Administration to brother and
    next of kin Walter Blagrave. (Nov. 1678).
Blagrave, Thomas, of Westminster. (Kinswoman Anne Williams in
    Virginia). Probate to relict Margaret Blagrave. (Dec. 1688).
Blake, John, of Minehead, Somerset, who died at Virginia.
    Administration to nephew Hugh Saffin. (May 1663).
Bland, Edward, of Virginia, bachelor. Administration to brother
    John Bland. (July 1652).
Bland, John, of St. Olave Hart Street, London. (Wife Sarah
    Bland in Virginia). Probate to Thomas Povey with similar
    powers reserved to relict Sarah Bland. (June 1680). Wa.
Blaydes, Samuel, of Virginia, bachelor. Administration to
    principal creditor Richard Booth. (June 1683).
Blisse, Mary, of Virginia. Administration to sister Martha,
    wife of John Ward. (Nov. 1655).
Bludder, Thomas, of Clewer, Berkshire. (Kin in Virginia).
    Probate to relict Emma Bludder. (1654).
Bly, John, who died overseas (in Virginia). Probate to brother
    Giles Bly. (May 1664). Sm.Wi.
Boddy, John, of Stepney, Middlesex, who died at Maryland.
    Administration to relict Camelia Boddy. (June 1683).
Bolles, John, of Clerkenwell, Middlesex. (Brother Joseph Bolles
    in New England). Probate to John Sparrow and Joseph Clarke.
    (May 1666). Wa.
Bolton, Philip, of St. Leonard Eastcheap, London, who died in
    Virginia. Administration to brother Thomas Bolton. (June
    1673). Inventory PROB4/9998.

Bolton, William, of Harrow on the Hill, Middlesex, clerk.
(Brother Henry Bolton in Virginia). Probate to Robert
Payne with similar powers reserved to Thomas Robinson.
(Feb. 1692). Wa.

Bond, Richard, of Bristol, who died at Virginia or overseas.
Administration to Margaret Bird, aunt of children William,
George, Richard and Mary Bond during their minority. (Aug.
1652). See NGSQ 62/203.

Booteflower, John, of Stepney, Middlesex, who died in Virginia.
Administration to principal creditor Edmund Bugden; relict
Margaret Booteflower renouncing. (Apr. 1663).

Booth, John, of Stepney, Middlesex, who died on ship *Industry*
at Virginia. Probate to relict Sarah Booth. (Apr. 1694).

Booth, William, of Wapping, Stepney, Middlesex, who died at
Virginia, bachelor. Administration to father William Booth.
(Jan. 1676).

Boreman, Thomas, of Virginia, bachelor. Administration to uncle
Sir William Boreman. (Jan. 1679).

Bossinger, Thomas, of New England who died on ship *Elizabeth*.
Administration to Edward Hull, attorney for relict Mary
Bossinger during her absence. (June 1698).

Boughton, Robert, of New England, bachelor. Administration to
father Robert Boughton. (Jan. 1656).

Bower, Thomas, of Dover, Kent, who died at New England, bachelor.
Administration to brother William Bower. (Jan. 1659).

Bowman, John, of Stepney, Middlesex, who died in Virginia.
Limited administration to principal creditor Richard Cox,
merchant of London, with consent of relict Sarah Bowman.
(Dec. 1691).

Bowman, Thomas, of Stepney, Middlesex, who died on ship *Henry*
at Virginia. Administration to relict Joanne Bowman. (June
1694).

Boxe, Tobias, who died abroad (with goods in Virginia). Probate
to Agnes Barber. (Dec. 1629). Wi.

Boys, John, who died abroad (bound for Virginia). Probate to
uncle ------ Boys and Thomas Major. (May 1650). Sm.Wa.

Boys, Thomas, of Patochanick River, Virginia, widower. Administration to son Thomas Boys. (Aug. 1656).

Boys, William, of Cranbrook, Kent. (Kinsmen Thomas and John
Stow in New England). Probate to relict Joane Boys. (Feb.
1657).

Bracegirdle, John, of London who died at Virginia, bachelor.
Administration to brother Joseph Bracegirdle. (Nov. 1673).

Braddock, Nathaniel, formerly of Norwich but who died abroad,
(bound for Virginia). Administration to brother John Braddock.
(Mar. 1636). Revoked on production of will and probate
granted to brother-in-law John Rooke. (May 1636). Wa.Wi.

Bradford, Thomas, of Batcombe, Somerset, who died in Virginia,
bachelor. Administration to principal creditor John Boreman.
(Nov. 1671).

Brading, Nathaniel, who died abroad bound to East Indies.
(Uncle Richard Kent of Newberry, New England). Probate to
father William Brading. (July 1648). Sh.Wa.

Bradley, Daniel, of Gosport, Hampshire, who died in Virginia.
Administration to relict Margery Bradley. (Dec. 1669).

Brand, John, of ship *Prince* who died at Virginia, bachelor.
Administration by decree to principal creditor Patrick
Hopbourne during absence of father Alexander Brand. (July
1676).

Bray, Richard, of Rappahannock River, Virginia. Administration
to sister Elianor Daniell. (Nov. 1691).

Breedon, Zacheus, who died at sea or abroad, (bound for
   Carolina or Maryland), bachelor. Probate to Laurence
   Stevenson. (Sept. 1686). Wa.
Brent, Edward, who died overseas, (goods in Virginia). Probate
   to Edward Willett, attorney for brother Giles Brent with
   similar powers reserved to brother John Brent. (Aug. 1625).
   Wa.
Bretland, Elizabeth, of Barbados, widow. (Brother Adam Coulson
   of New England). Probate to Edward Munday and John Mortimer.
   (Dec. 1690). Wa.
Brett, Sir Edward, of Bexley, Kent, who died at St. Margaret,
   Westminster, Middlesex. (Nephew Henry Isham of Virginia).
   Probate to Stephen Beckingham and Richard Watson. (Mar.
   1684). Wa.
Brett, John, of St. Andrew Undershaft, London. (Lands in New
   England). Probate to son John Brett. (Jan. 1686). Wa.
Brewer, John, citizen and grocer of London who died in Virginia.
   Administration with will to relict Mary Brewer alias Butler
   during minority of children John, Roger and Margaret Brewer.
   (May 1636). Sh.Wa.
Bridge alias Bridges, John, of Virginia. Administration to
   kinsman George Warren. (Mar. 1637).
Bridges, Francis, of Clapham, Surrey. (Bequests to friends in
   Virginia). Probate to relict Sarah Bridges. (June 1642).
   Sh.
Brighouse, James, of Virginia, bachelor. Administration to
   mother Elizabeth Brighouse. (June 1683).
Brightwell, Charles, of Virginia, bachelor. Administration to
   principal creditor Thomas Darling. (Aug. 1660).
Brinley, Thomas, of Datchet, Buckinghamshire. (Daughter
   Grissell, wife of Nathaniel Silvester in New England).
   Probate to relict Anne Brinley. (Dec. 1661) Wa.
Britten, John, of Hadleigh, Suffolk, (adventurer to Virginia).
   Probate to son Laurence Britten. (Feb. 1637). Wi.
Broadhurst, Hugh, who died at Virginia, bachelor. Admini-
   stration to brother John Broadhurst. (June 1659).
Broadribb, John, of Chester River, Talbot Co., Maryland in West
   Indies. Administration to Charles Cottle, father of next
   of kin, nephew by a sister, John Cottle, during his minority.
   (July 1687).
Brookesbancke, Isaac, of ship *Anne* who died at sea or overseas,
   (bound for Maryland). Probate to brother William Brookes-
   bancke. (Aug. 1675).
Brooks, John, of Stepney, Middlesex, who died at Virginia.
   Administration to relict Mary Brooks. (July 1684).
Broome, Thomas, of H.M.S. *Dunkirk*, bachelor, (bound from Lee-
   ward Islands to Boston). Administration with will to John
   Aldred, attorney for executor Francis Ward now in distant
   parts. (June 1695).
Browne, John, of St. Michael Bassishaw, London, who died in
   Virginia. Administration to relict Susan Parrott alias Browne.
   (Oct. 1668).
Browne, Moses, of St. Margaret Lothbury, London. (Sister Sarah
   Noyse of New England). Probate to Benjamin Wilkes, Richard
   Browne and Richard Ventham. (June 1688). Wa.
Browne, Sarah, of Gloucester, widow. (Grandchild Sarah, wife
   of William Barnes in New England). Probate to Gregory
   Wilshire. (Dec. 1646). Wa. See NGSQ 61/115.
Browne, Thomas, of Plymouth, Devon, (goods in New England).
   Administration with will to relict Priscilla Browne; no
   executor having been named. (July 1663). Wa.

Browne, Thomas, of fireship *Hart* who died at New England,
bachelor. Probate to brother George Browne with similar
powers reserved to Theophilus Rabneere, John Dagger and
Joseph Store; administration granted previous month to
mother Margaret Browne revoked. (Nov. 1693).

Browne, William, of Ratcliffe, Middlesex, who died in Virginia.
Administration to relict Anne Browne. (May 1657).

Browne, William, of Plymouth, Devon, who died in Virginia,
widower. Administration to principal creditor William
Clarke. (June 1668).

Browninge, William, of Virginia. Administration to uncle John
Browninge. (Sept. 1651).

Brownsford, James, of Virginia. Administration to principal
creditor Tristram Bartlett; brother and sister John and
Susan Brownsford renouncing. (Aug. 1684).

Brumpsted, Rose, of St. Martin in Fields, Middlesex, spinster.
(Kinsman Thomas Breedon in New England). Administration
with will to Thomas Brumpsted, father of principal legatees
Thomas and Charles Brumpsted; executors John Bredon, Edward
Edgins and Edward Noell renouncing. (July 1666). Wa.

Bugge, Rev. Nathaniel, of Brandeston, Suffolk. (Kinsman Thomas
Bugge in Virginia). Probate to brother Joseph Bugge.
(Apr. 1656). Wi.

Bulkeley, Arthur, of London, merchant, (bound for Virginia).
Probate to brother Thomas Bulkeley. (Nov. 1645). Sh.Wi.

Bulkeley, John, of St. Katherine by the Tower, London.
(Brother Thomas Bulkeley of New England). Probate to
Edward and Avis Bulkeley and Elizabeth Faulkner. (Jan. 1690).
Wa.

Bullen, Thomas, of Virginia, bachelor. Administration to
brother Arthur Bullen. (May 1690).

Bullocke, Hugh, of All Hallows, Barking, London. (Son William
Bullocke in Virginia). Administration with will to principal creditor Samuel Burrell; executor John Limbry having
died. (Nov. 1650). Wi.

Bullocke, William, of Barking, Essex, (bound for Virginia).
Probate to relict Elizabeth Bullocke. (May 1650). Sh.Wi.

Burbridge alias Burges alias Church, Elizabeth, of St. Giles in
Fields, Middlesex, widow. Administration to Charles Raven,
husband of sister Mary Nicholas alias Raven, in New England.
(Nov. 1687). Revoked and granted to Anne Yeates, widow,
guardian of nephews and niece by a brother, Sarah, Samuel
and John Church during the absence of Mary Nicholas alias
Raven. (Dec. 1687).

Burges, John the elder, of Westley, Devon., (sick in New England).
Probate to relict Joanna Burges alias Bray. (May 1628).
Sh.Wa.

Burges, Joseph, of Marlborough, Wiltshire, (and late of Maryland),
who died in City of London, merchant. Probate to John Keynes.
(Nov. 1672). Wa.

Burges, William, of South River, Anne Arundell Co., Maryland.
Administration with will to Micajah Perry, attorney for
relict Ursula, now wife of Mordecai Moore at Anne Arundell Co.
(July 1689). Wa.

Burnapp, John, of Aston, Hertfordshire. (Son Thomas Burnapp in
New England). Probate to son John Burnapp. (Mar. 1654). Wa.

Burnell, Thomas, citizen and clothworker of London. (Nephew
John Morley of New England). Probate to relict Hester
Burnell. (Oct. 1661). Wa.

Burrell, William, of Virginia. Probate to brother-in-law
Richard Kelley. (Aug. 1648). Sh.Wa.Wi.

Burrell, William, of Stepney, Middlesex, who died in Virginia
on ship *Mary*. Administration to relict Hannah Burrell.
(Jan. 1692).

Burrough, Nathaniel, of Limehouse, Stepney, Middlesex. (Son
George Burrough in New England). Probate to Anne Wheeler.
(Mar. 1683). Wa.

Burrowes, John, of Bristol who died at Virginia. Administration to principal creditrix Frances Hobbs; relict Deborah
Burrowes renouncing. (Feb. 1691).

Burton, George, who died overseas, (bound to New England),
bachelor. Administration with will to brother John Burton
and to John Ellis, both of St. Clement Danes, Middlesex.
(Feb. 1637). Sh.

Burton, Richard, of Virginia, bachelor. Administration to
sisters Elizabeth Vaughan alias Cooke, wife of Hugh Vaughan,
and Martha Cooke, spinster. (Oct. 1656).

Burton, Richard, of Virginia. Administration to daughter Anne,
wife of George Coombe. (Dec. 1656).

Burton, Thomas, of New England who died on ship *Quaker Ketch*.
Administration to father Abraham Burton during absence in
New England of relict Susan Burton. (Feb. 1689).

Butcher, Thomas, of Wadhurst, Sussex. (Kinswoman Margaret,
wife of Thomas Swanne, in Virginia). Probate to relict
Mary Butcher. (Sept. 1646). Revoked on her death and
administration granted to her husband Henry Dyke. (Nov.
1651). Wi.

Butler, George, of Maryland. Administration to principal
creditrix Jane Cooper; relict Margaret Butler renouncing.
(Oct. 1698).

Butler, John the elder, of Conecchocut, New England. Administration to principal creditor Phillip Frensh; relict Mary
and children John, William and Alexander Butler renouncing.
(Dec. 1698 and Jan. 1699).

Butler, Stephen, of New England who died on ship *John* of London
at Sierra Leone, Gambia. Administration to Benjamin Burges
of Stepney, Middlesex, shipwright, cousin and only next of
kin in England of relict Tabitha Butler. (Nov. 1694).

Butler, Thomas, who died overseas, (Minister of God's word;
expecting tobacco from Virginia). Probate to relict Mary
Butler. (July 1637). Wi.

Cade, Andrew, of East Betchworth, Surrey. (Cousin Henry Cade
in Virginia). Probate to relict Magdalen Cade. (Oct. 1662).
Wi.

Caffinch, John, of Tenterden, Kent, (late of New Haven, New
England). Probate to Samuel Caffinch. (Jan. 1659). Wa.

Cage, Gilbert, of ship *Hopewell* who died at Virginia. Administration to Sarah, wife of principal creditor Andrew Boswell
during his absence overseas; relict Mary Cage renouncing.
(July 1680).

Calvert, George, (of St. Mary's, Maryland), who died overseas.
Probate to William Peasely with similar powers reserved to
brother Leonard Calvert. (Jan. 1635). Sh.

Campbell, William, of Wapping, Middlesex, who died on ship
  Anne at Virginia. Probate by sentence to David ------?
  (Nov. 1693).
Carew, Nicholas, of St. Martin in Fields, Middlesex. (Lands in
  Maryland). Probate to brother Swithin Carew. (Oct. 1670).
  Wa.
Carleton, Arthur, of Merryland, widower. Administration to
  brother Matthew Carleton; mother Margaret Carleton renouncing.
  (July 1681).
Carpender, Francis, formerly of City of London but late of
  Hereford. (Cousin Simon Carpender in Virginia). Probate
  to relict Hellen Carpender. (May 1662).
Carpenter, William, of St. George's, Southwark, Surrey, who
  died at New York on H.M.S. *Richmond*. Probate to relict
  Elizabeth Carpenter. (July 1695).
Carr, Sir Robert, of Carr Island, New England, who died in
  Bristol. Administration with will to son William Carr; no
  executor having been named. (July 1667). Wa.
Carter, Edward, of Edmonton, Middlesex. (Lands in Virginia).
  Probate to relict Elizabeth Carter. (Nov. 1682). Wa.
Carter, Elizabeth - see Lloyd.
Carter, Evans, of ship *Rose* who died at Boston, New England,
  bachelor. Administration to principal creditor Phillip
  Martin. (Feb. 1691).
Carter, James, of Whitechapel, Middlesex. (Lands in Virginia).
  Probate to relict Susan Carter. (Apr. 1627). Wa.
Carter, James (*John* in Probate Act Book), of Hinderclay,
  Suffolk. (Son Thomas Carter in New England). Administra-
  tion with will to relict Mary Carter. (Oct. 1655). Wa.
Carter, John, of Whitechapel, Middlesex. (Brother Robert
  Skelton of New York). Probate to Samuel Sheppard and
  Samuel Perry. (June 1692). Wa.
Carteret, Sir George. (Lands in New Jersey). Probate to
  relict Dame Elizabeth Carteret. (Feb. 1680). Wa.
Carwithen, David, of Boston, New England, who died on H.M.S.
  Crownation. Administration to William Dibbs, attorney for
  relict Elizabeth Carwithen at Boston. "Pauper." (Jan. 1695).
Carwithen, Digery, of New England. Administration to relict
  Eleanor Carwithen. (July 1653).
Cary, Alice, of Shadwell, Stepney, Middlesex, spinster. (Uncle
  Miles Cary of Virginia). Probate to Richard and Dorothy Cary.
  (Nov. 1660). Wa.
Cary, Richard, of Barbados, merchant. (Goods in New York).
  Probate to Samuel and William Cary and Damaris Berriff.
  (Aug. 1685). Wa.
Cawood, Elizabeth, of Boston, New England, widow. Administra-
  tion to daughter Mary, wife of John Smith. (July 1693).
Chalfont, Margaret, of St. Sepulchre, London, widow. (Sister
  Susanna Harris of New England). Probate to surviving executor
  Sarah Norris. (Oct. 1678). Wa.
Chambrelan, Peter the elder, of St. Dionis Backchurch, London,
  surgeon. (Bequest to Robert Smith in Virginia). Probate
  to Abraham Chambrelan with similar powers reserved to Richard
  Legge. (Dec. 1631). Wi.
Chambers, William, of Virginia, bachelor. Administration to
  father George Chambers. (Apr. 1670).
Chambers, William, of Stepney, Middlesex, who died in Carolina.
  Administration to relict Susan Chambers. (Apr. 1683).
Chandler, Edward, of Ware, Hertfordshire. (Son Daniel Chandler
  and daughter Sarah Chandler in Virginia). Probate to relict
  Elizabeth Chandler and son Edward Chandler. (Apr. 1651).
  Sh.Wi.

Chapell, William, of Stepney, Middlesex, who died at Virginia.
Administration to relict Uritha Chapell. (Nov. 1682).
Chaplen, Moses, of St. Mary's, Guildford, Surrey. (Cousin
Ester Pierce the elder in New England). Probate to mother
and father Moses and Collett Chaplen. (Aug. 1669). Revoked
on their death and administration granted to brother William
Chaplen. (Jan. 1671). Wa.
Chaplin, Clement, of Thetford, Norfolk, clerk. (Lands in New
England). Probate to relict Sarah Chaplin. (Sept. 1656). Wa.
Charlett, Richard, (of Calvert Co., Maryland), who died at sea
or abroad. Probate to Richard Kings. (Apr. 1694). Wa.
Charter, Andrew, of Wapping, Middlesex, who died on ship *Edward
and Francis* at Virginia, bachelor. Administration to father
Richard Charter. (Apr. 1694).
Chauncy, Judith, of Yardley, Hertfordshire, spinster. (Brother
Charles Chauncy in New England). Probate to Henry Chauncy
and Montague Lane. (Mar. 1658). Sh.Wa.
Cheesman, John, of Virginia. Administration to father John
Cheesman during minority of daughters Margaret and Anne
Cheesman. (Sept. 1661).
Cheeseman, John, of Bermondsey, Surrey. (Lands in Virginia).
Probate to relict Margaret Cheeseman. (May 1665). Sh.Wi.
Cheeseman, Margaret, of Bermondsey, Surrey, widow. (Kinsmen
Lemuel Mason, Elizabeth Theleball and John Matthews of
Virginia). Probate to Margaret Mason. (July 1680). Wa.
Chesley, Phillip, of York Co., Virginia. Probate to relict
Margaret Chesley. (May 1675). Wi.
Chetwood, Jane, of West Felton, Shropshire. (Sister Grace, wife
of Peter Bulkley of New England). Probate to sister Abigail
Chetwood with similar powers reserved to Edward Jones and
----- Powell. (Dec. 1648). Wa.
Cheyney, Anne, of St. Katherine Creechurch, London. (Cousin
Anne Roe in Virginia). Probate to John Gray. (Oct. 1667). Wi.
Church, Elizabeth - see Burbridge.
Clarke, Agnes, of Ashill, Somerset, widow. (Kinsman William
Harvey in New England). Probate to kinsman Richard Harvey.
(May 1648). Sh.Wa.
Clarke, Andrew, of St. Sepulchre, London, who died at Maryland.
Administration with will to brother Andrew *(sic)* Clarke;
named executor Robert Johnson renouncing. (Apr. 1691).
Clarke, James, of Little Towne, Virginia, bachelor. Administra-
tion to brother and sister John Clarke and Elizabeth, wife
of Richard Warner, pending production of will. (Sept. 1658).
Clarke alias Kingman, John, of Wells, Somerset. (Son James
Clarke in New England). Probate to son Samuel Clarke alias
Kingman. (Sept. 1641). Wa.
Clarke, Richard, of Virginia. Administration to daughter Mar-
garet, wife of John Howard. (Aug. 1686).
Clarke, Robert, of Rotherhithe, Surrey, who died overseas,
(of New England). Administration with will to Walter Rogers
guardian of son John Clarke during his minority. (Mar. 1663).
Marginal note: "Revoked on deathof Walter Rogers, Mar. 1663."
Clarke, Robert, of St. Giles, Cripplegate, London, (late of
Maryland). Probate to John Clarke with similar powers
reserved to Jane Clarke. (Dec. 1689).
Clarke, Thomas, of York, Virginia. Probate to Peter Temple.
(May 1670). Wi.
Clarke, William, of ship *Kings Fisher* who died at Boston, New
England. Administration to principal creditor Thomas Long.
(Nov. 1687).
Cleare, Ambrose, of Great Stratton, New Kent Co., Virginia.
Administration with will to Richard Parke, merchant, attorney
for relict Anne, now wife of Thomas Tea at Virginia. (Nov.1697).

Clymer alias Ennis, Anne, of Maryland. Administration to
    cousin and next of kin Christopher Rayner. (Apr. 1691).
Cobb, Arthur, of parts overseas, (bound for Syranum, America).
    Probate to brother James Cobb. (Apr. 1666).
Coffin, Gregory, of Stepney, Middlesex, mariner, (bound for
    New England). Probate to John Earle. (Aug. 1662). Wa.
Coggeshall, Anne, of Castle Hedingham, Essex, widow. (Son
    John Coggeshall in New England). Probate to granddaughter
    Anne Raymond. (Nov. 1648). Wa.
Coke, John, of Dorchester. (Goods in New England). Probate
    to Gilbert Ironside, clerk, Edward Bragg and Richard Scovile
    with similar powers reserved to Thomas Gollopp and James
    Gould. (Oct. 1641). Wa.
Colcutt, William, of ship *Planter* who died in Virginia, widower.
    Administration with nuncupative will to Anne West, aunt and
    guardian of cousin Patience Dand; no executor having been
    named. (Aug. 1659).
Cole, Edward, of East Bergholt, Suffolk. (Grandchildren in
    New England). Probate to daughters Sarah and Mary Cole.
    (May 1652). Wa.
Cole, George, of Dorchester. (Lands in New England). Probate
    to relict Ann Cole and son John Cole. (May 1659). Wa.
Cole, John, of Weymouth and Melcombe Regis, Dorset, merchant.
    (Lands in New England). Probate to James Gold with similar
    powers reserved to Benjamin Speering. (Oct. 1672). Wa.
Cole, Jone, of Exeter, spinster *(sic)*. (Husband John Cole
    intended for Philadelphia). Probate to James Kearle.
    (Feb. 1694). Wa.
Cole(s), John, of Exeter who died overseas (Pennsylvania).
    Probate to James Kerle. (Oct. 1693).
Cole, Simon, of Boston, New England, who died at sea, bachelor.
    Administration to sister Mary Mervin. (Nov. 1674).
Cole, Walter, of Lavenham, Suffolk. (Daughter Elizabeth, wife
    of John Fuller in New England). Probate to relict Susan
    Cole. (Sept. 1653). Wa.
Colleton, Sir Peter, of St. James, Westminster, Middlesex.
    (Lands in Carolina). Probate to daughter Catherine Colleton
    with similar powers reserved to William Thornburgh; executor
    Colonel John Leslie having died overseas. (Apr. 1694).
    Double probate to William Thornburgh. (Nov. 1697). Wa.
Collyer, Joseph the elder, of St. Saviour, Southwark, Surrey.
    (Sister Mary Browninge in New England). Probate to sons
    Benjamin and Joseph Collyer. (Sept. 1649). Wa.
Collington, Edward, of St. Saviour, Southwark, Surrey, joiner.
    (Daughter Isabell in New England). Probate to relict Perrin
    Collington. (July 1660). Wa.
Collins, Richard, of Bristol who died in Virginia, bachelor.
    Administration to principal creditor Walter Stephens.
    (Aug. 1667).
Collins, Thomas, citizen and barber surgeon of London. (Sister
    Anne Collins alias Seaward in Virginia). Probate to son
    Phillip Collins. (Oct. 1657). Wi.
Collyer - see Collier.
Coltman, Anna, of Christ Church, Newgate, London. (Son in
    Virginia). Probate to Ralph Canninge. (Aug. 1623). Wa.
Coltman, William, of Virginia, (of Wapping, Middlesex in Caveat
    Book). Probate to mother Alice Coltman. (Nov. 1666).
Colvill, John, of Cranbrook, Kent. (Nephew John Colvill in
    New England). Probate to relict Susan Colvill. (July 1695).
Comer, Charles, of Stepney, Middlesex, who died at New York.
    Administration to relict Anne Comer. (May 1687).

Connell, John, of Younghall, Ireland, who died at Virginia,
    bachelor. Administration to Anne, wife of principal creditor
    William Peeters now at sea. (July 1675).
Connington, William, of Baltimore Co., Maryland, bachelor.
    Administration to brother Walter Connington. (July 1676).
Cooke, James, of Virginia, bachelor. Administration to sisters
    Elizabeth, wife of Hugh Vaughan, and Martha Cooke. (Oct. 1656).
Cooke, John, of Sprowston, Norfolk. (Bequest to Anne, wife of
    Edmund Pitts in New England). Probate to relict Elizabeth
    Cooke. (Nov. 1654). Wa.
Cooke, Samuel, of Dublin, Ireland. Probate to brother Erasmus
    Cooke and Thomas Cooke of London, goldsmith, with similar
    powers reserved to kinsman Clement Chaplyn of New England
    and Tobias Norris. (Sept. 1642). Sh.
Cooke, Samuel, of Rotherhithe, Surrey, who died at Virginia,
    bachelor. Administration to Dorothy Cooke, attorney for
    brother Miles Cooke overseas. (Oct. 1686).
Cooper, John, of Weston Hall, Warwickshire. (Brother Timothy
    Cooper in New England). Probate to relict Elizabeth Cooper.
    (Oct. 1655). Sh.Wa.
Cooper, Justinian, of Virginia. Administration to uncle William
    Cooper. (Sept. 1655).
Conners, John, who died at sea, (money in Virginia). Probate
    to relict Susannah Conners. (May 1654). Sh.Wa.
Copp, Anthony, of Honeley, Warwickshire. (Brother William Copp
    in New England). Probate to brother Walter Copp. (June 1654).
    Wa.
Corderoy, William, of parts overseas (Virginia), bachelor.
    Probate to brother Jasper Corderoy. (Oct. 1667).
Corneforth, Leonard, of Stepney, Middlesex, who died in Virginia.
    Administration to Elizabeth, wife of principal creditor John
    Marsingham during his absence abroad; relict Catherine
    Corneforth renouncing. (May 1681).
Cornelison, Hanse alias John, of Virginia, bachelor. Admini-
    stration to principal creditor Andrew Anderson. (Nov. 1682).
Cornish, John, of Ottery St. Mary, Devon, who died at New England,
    bachelor. Administration to principal creditor Henry Marker.
    (Feb. 1695).
Cornwell, Thomas, of London who died at Maryland, bachelor.
    Administration with will to brother Anthony Cornwell; named
    executor John Turner renouncing. (Dec. 1695).
Cotchett, Robert, of Mickleover, Derbyshire. (Sister Dorothy,
    wife of John Joyce of New England). Probate to relict Anne
    Cochett. (Apr. 1658). Sh.
Couch, Ralph, of Stepney, Middlesex, who died at Virginia.
    Administration to principal creditor Benjamin Dennis. (Sept.
    1676).
Coward, William, of Boston, New England, who died in King's
    service on ship *Neptune*. Administration with will to relict
    Christine Coward; no executor having been named. (Oct. 1691).
Cox, James, of Bristol who died at Maryland, bachelor. Admini-
    stration to father Christopher Cox. (Feb. 1680).
Cox, Margery, of Deptford, Kent, widow. (Brother Giles Webb in
    Virginia). Probate to Mary Waight with similar powers
    reserved to Elizabeth Waight. (June 1656). Wa.
Cox, Thomas, of Nansy Mumm, Virginia, bachelor. Administration
    to father Richard Cox. (June 1697). Revoked on his death
    and granted to sister Mary Tinkerson alias Cox. (Mar. 1698).
Crabbe, Osmond, of Brislington, Somerset. (Brother John Crabbe
    in Virginia). Administration with will to sister Alice Vaughan;
    executors Sir William Hayman and William Swimmer renouncing.
    (Apr. 1695). Wi.

Crabb, Samuel, of New England who died at Stepney, Middlesex,
bachelor. Administration with nuncupative will to William
Marsh; no executor having been named. (Sept. 1694).
Cradock, Mathew, of St. Swithin, London. (Goods in New England).
Probate to relict Rebecca Cradock. (June 1641). Sh.
Crane, Robert, of Great Coggeshall, Essex. (Daughter wife of
Nathaniel Rogers of New England). Probate to Samuel Crane.
(Mar. 1659). Wa.
Crane, Robert, of Hadleigh, Suffolk. (Aunt Rogers in New
England). Probate to sister Mary, wife of Lawrence Stisted.
(May 1669). Wa.
Crane, Samuel, of Great Coggeshall, Essex. (Cousin John Rogers
in New England). Probate to William Cox the elder and Isaac
Hubberd. (Aug. 1670). Wa.
Crane, Thomas, of Kelvedon, Essex. (Sister Margaret, wife of
Nathaniel Rogers in New England). Probate to Robert Crane
and Henry Whiteing, guardians of children Robert and Mary
Crane during their minority. (Mar. 1655). Wa.
Creed, John, of Martyn's Hundred, Virginia. Administration
with will to Anne, wife of Thomas Faussett during his absence
in Virginia. (Apr. 1635). Sh.Wi.
Creffield, Edward the younger, who died at sea, merchant.
(Daughter-in-law Lucy, wife of Thomas Reed of Gloucester,
Virginia). Probate to Philip Richards with similar powers
reserved to Benjamin Clements. (Dec. 1694). Wi.
Crego, Stephen, of New York who died on H.M.S. *Archangel*.
Administration to John Corbett, attorney for relict Margery
Crego in New York. (May 1692).
Crewes, James, of Virginia, widower. Administration to daughter
Sarah Whittingham. (Sept. 1677).
Croke, Paulus Ambrosius, of Hasleigh, Essex, (intending for
Virginia). Probate to uncle John Nevell. (Aug. 1652). Wa.
Crooke, Thomas, (of London, bound for Virginia), who died abroad.
Probate to father Thomas Crooke. (June 1681). Wi.
Crosse, Samuel, of St. Saviour, Southwark, Surrey. (Credits
in Boston, New England). Probate to relict Mary Crosse.
(June 1667).
Crosse, William, of Blandford, Dorset, who died in Maryland,
widower. Administration to principal creditor Richard Draper.
(Mar. 1683).
Crouch, Richard, of St. Giles Cripplegate, London. (Brother
William Crouch in New England). Probate to relict Anne
Crouch. (Nov. 1660). Wa.
Crumpe, Mary - see Harris.
Cubitt, Robert, of Virginia, bachelor. Administration to sister
Sarah Cubitt. (Feb. 1675).
Cully, Abraham, of Stafford Co., Virginia, bachelor. Limited
administration with will to brother John Cully. (Apr. 1694).
Curtyce, John, of Burghfield, Berkshire. (Sister Jane, wife of
Thomas Collyer in New England). Probate to John Curtis of
Tilehurst, John Curtis of Tadley, John Go--- of London,
merchant, and James Maynard of Reading, wool drawer. (Oct.1660).
Curtis, John, of Virginia, bachelor. Administration to brother
Alexander Curtis. (Aug. 1684).
Curtis, John, (of Boston, New England) who died on H.M.S.
English Tyger, bachelor. Probate to Robert Chipchase.
(Dec. 1680). Wa.
Custis, Joseph, of Kingston upon Hull, Yorkshire, who died at
Accomack, Virginia. Administration by decree to principal
creditor Edward Miles. (Feb. 1656). Revoked and granted to
son Zachary Custis. (July 1685).

Cuthbertson, William, of ship *Elizabeth and Catherine* who
died in Virginia, bachelor. Administration to nephew
William Cuthbertson. (June 1678).

Cutt, Richard, of Portsmouth in Piscataqua in parts overseas.
Probate to relict Elianor Cutt and daughters Margaret,
wife of William Vaughan, and Bridget, wife of Thomas
Daniel. (July 1682). Wa.

Dale, Dame Elizabeth, of Westminster, Middlesex, widow.
Lands in Virginia). Probate to Richard Hamby and William
Shrimpton. (Dec. 1640). Wa.

Daniell, Nicholas, of Stepney, Middlesex, Captain of ship
Hampshire, who died at Virginia. Administration to relict
Mary Daniell. (Mar. 1694).

Darby, Agnes, of Bisley, Surrey, widow. (Kinsman Edward
Darby in New England). Probate to Henry Collier. (June
1650). Sh.Wa.

Dauncey, Joseph, chaplain of ship *Falcon*. Administration to
Samuel Wallin, father of relict Anne Myles alias Dauncey
in New England. (Jan. 1699).

Davies, Isaack, of Virginia, bachelor. Administration to
father Thomas Davies. (Dec. 1658).

Davis, Jonathan, of Barne Elms, Surrey, who died in Virginia.
Administration to son Jonathan Davis; relict Mary Davis
renouncing. (Mar. 1684). Revoked on his death and granted
to relict Mary Davis. (Oct. 1697).

Davies, Richard, of Virginia. Probate to relict Joanne Davies.
(July 1661), Wi.

Davis, William, of New York, who died on ketch *Aldborough*.
Probate to relict Elianor Davis. (Aug. 1694).

Davy, John, of Maidstone, Kent, who died in London.
(Nephew John Davy in Virginia). Probate to daughters
Mary Wall and Elizabeth Andrewes. (June 1649). Wa.

Dawkins, Simon, of Petsworth, Hampshire, who died at Long
Island near New England, bachelor. Administration to
brother and next of kin John Dawkins. (June 1675).

Day, John, of Rotherhithe, Surrey, who died overseas. (Goods
in Virginia). Administration to relict Anne Day. (Apr.
1672).

Deacon, Thomas, of St. Saviour, Southwark, Surrey. (Cousin
Thomas Deacon in Virginia). Probate to relict Margaret
Deacon. (Oct. 1652). Wi.

Deane, George, (of New England), who died at Barbados on ship
Princess Anne, bachelor. Administration with will to
Henry Wilke; no executor having been named. (Dec. 1693).
Wa.

Deane, Thomas, of Fryvoke, Hampshire, (and formerly of Boston,
New England). Probate to brother John Deane with similar
powers reserved to William Browne. (May 1686). Revoked o
death of John Deane and administration granted to his son
Thomas Deane; William Browne renouncing. (Apr. 1695). Wa.

De Lavall, Thomas, of New York City. Administration with will
to Thomas Landon, attorney for son John De Lavall now overseas. (Feb. 1683).

Delawne, Gideon, of Blackfriars, London. (Lands in Virginia).
   Probate to relict Jane Delawne. (Jan. 1659). Wa.
Deledicq, Lawrence, of ship *Bever* (bound for New York), who
   died overseas. Probate to Paul Ray. (Oct. 1691).
Delke alias Kenythorpe, Elizabeth, who died in Virginia, widow.
   Administration to sister Catherine Kenythorpe. (June 1629).
Derickson, George, of Shadwell, Middlesex, who died at Virginia
   in ship *Unicorne*, bachelor. Administration with will to
   Anne, wife and attorney of Thomas Anderson now overseas.
   (June 1685).
Derickson, Harman, of Virginia, bachelor. Administration to
   Barbara, wife and attorney of principal creditor Stephen
   Johnson during his absence. (July 1676).
Derrick, Henry, of St. Stephen's, Bristol, who died in Virginia,
   (now resident in Virginia). Probate to relict Sarah Derrick.
   (Oct. 1677). Wi.
Dewar, John, of St. Michael, Crooked Lane, London, who died at
   Quitto, Virginia, bachelor. Administration to principal
   creditor Raphael Whistler. (June 1686).
Dewell, Edward, of Warwick Squeak, Virginia, who died overseas.
   Probate to Simon Curnocke; administration as of intestate
   granted to brother Humphrey Dewell in June 1637 revoked.
   (Nov. 1640). Sh.Wi.
Dewin, Richard, of St. Botolph Aldgate, London. (Kinswoman
   Sarah Cowley in Virginia). Probate to relict Alice Dewin.
   (Sept. 1647). Wi.
Dickeson, Andrew, of St. Mary Magdalene, Bermondsey, Surrey,
   who died at Virginia, bachelor. Administration to principal
   creditor Mary Willys. (Aug. 1681).
Dickenson, Michael, of Altringham, Cheshire. (Nephew James
   Talier in Virginia). Probate to Michael Colley with similar
   powers reserved to Hugh Colley. (May 1698).
Dickinson, Francis, of Northam, Devon, mariner, bound to
   Virginia. Administration with will to Richard Draper,
   uncle of Laurence and Philip Dickinson during their minority.
   (Sept. 1630).
Diggs, Edward, of Virginia. Probate to relict Elizabeth Diggs.
   (June 1686). Wi.
Dixon, Jonas, who died at Virginia on ship *Preservation*.
   Probate to Sarah Yates with similar powers reserved to
   Richard Yates. (Mar. 1699).
Dixon, Miles, of Virginia. Administration to brother Robert
   Dixon. (July 1660).
Dickson, William, of Virginia, bachelor. Administration to
   brother Robert Dickson. (Oct. 1686).
Dobson, Samuel, of New England, who died at Holborn, Middlesex,
   bachelor. Administration to principal creditor John Stevens.
   (Apr. 1690).
Dolbery, Andrew, of New England, who died in France, widower.
   Administration to niece by a sister Avis Coombes, spinster.
   (Aug. 1694).
Domelaw, Richard, who died overseas. (Goods in Virginia).
   Administration with will to brother John Domelaw. (Sept.
   1624). Sh.
Downe, Nicholas, of London. (Niece Joane Downe in Virginia).
   Probate to relict Ann Downe. (May. 1653). Sh.Wi.
Downing, John, of St. Clement Danes, Middlesex. (Daughter
   Abigail may go to Virginia). Probate to sons Richard and
   Francis Downing. (July 1623). Wa.
Drake, Francis, of Esher, Surrey. (Cousin John Drake to be
   sent to New England). Probate to son Francis Drake with
   similar powers reserved to John White. (May 1634). Wa.

Draper, Elizabeth, of St. Clement Eastcheap, London, widow.
(Son-in-law Abraham Peirsey in Virginia). Probate to
Thomas Guye, attorney for Richard Eerisford and Michael
Warryner. (Sept. 1625). Wi.
Dring, Stephen, of Deptford, Kent, who died at Virginia.
Administration to relict Patience Dring. (Mar. 1675).
Driver, William, of Virginia, bachelor. Administration to
father Edward Driver. (Apr. 1681).
Drumond, William, of Virginia. Administration to relict Sarah
Drumond. (Oct. 1677).
Drumont, James, of Virginia, bachelor. Probate to Christian
Mustard. (Feb. 1667).
Dudley, Thomas, of New England, bachelor. Administration to
father Joseph Dudley. (Nov. 1696).
Dummer, Thomas, of North Stoneham, Hampshire. (Daughter
Margaret Clements of New England). Probate to kinsmen John
and Stephen Dummer with similar powers reserved to Stephen
Penton. (Nov. 1650). Wa.
Duncombe, Susanna - see Johnson.
Dunn, John, of ship *Resolution* who died at sea, bachelor.
Administration to principal creditrix Margaret, wife of
Edward Pratt now in New England. (Sept. 1686).
Durford, William, of St. Saviour, Southwark, Surrey, who died
in Virginia. Administration to relict Elizabeth Durford.
(Sept. 1646).
Dyre, William, of Sussex Co., Pennsylvania. Probate to son
William Dyre with similar powers reserved to relict Mary
Dyre. (Sept. 1690). Wa.

Eades, John, of New England. Probate to George Hallam with
similar powers reserved to Winifred Hall. (Sept. 1698).
Eastall, William, of Virginia who died at sea. Administration
to relict Anne Mayo alias Eastall. (Jan. 1668).
Eaton, Benony, of Bermondsey, Surrey. (Lands in Virginia).
Probate to relict Deborah Eaton. (May 1677). Wi.
Eckley, John, of Philadelphia. Administration with will to
James Lewis, Peregrine Musgrave and Richard Stafford,
executors to relict Sarah Eckley deceased. (Feb. 1699).
Eckley, Sarah, of Philadelphia. Probate to James Lewis,
Peregrine Musgrave and Richard Stafford. (Dec. 1698).
Edmonds, James, of Boston, New England, bachelor. Administra-
tion to father Edward Edmonds. (June 1677).
Edmonds, John, formerly of Collingbourne Abbots, Wiltshire, but
who died at Virginia, bachelor. Probate to George Blanchard.
(July 1672).
Edwards, David, of Boston, New England. Probate to Edward Hill,
attorney for relict Mary Edwards in Boston. (July 1698).
Edwards, Henry, of ship *Dove* who died at Virginia. Administra-
tion to cousin german and next of kin Christopher Goulding.
(June 1656).
Edwards, John, of London who died in Virginia. (Lands in Vir-
ginia). Probate to Spencer Piggott. (Nov. 1668). Wi.
Eeles, Nathaniel, of Harpenden, Hertfordshire. (Son John Eeles
in Virginia). Probate to relict Sarah Eeles. (Feb. 1678). Wa.

Efford, Peter, of Newington, Surrey. (Lands in Virginia).
    Probate by decree to Rev. John Weldon and Albert Skinner.
    (Oct. 1665). Wi.
Elbridge, John, of Bristol, merchant. (Goods in New England).
    Probate to Nathaniel Cale with similar powers reserved to
    brother Thomas Elbridge. (Oct. 1646). Sh.Wa.
Eldred, William, of Bermondsey, Surrey, who died in Virginia.
    Administration to relict Ruth Eldred. (Mar. 1660).
    Revoked on her death and granted to daughter Sarah, wife of
    Iziaker Daldy now overseas. (Feb. 1683).
Elliot, George, who died overseas (bound for Virginia).
    Probate to Elizabeth Corbin. (July 1665).
Ellis, John, of Virginia. Probate to William Jordan with consent
    of brother Henry Ellis; similar powers reserved to Liveing
    Denwood, Richard Bayley and Stephen Horsey. (June 1659).
Elsam, Dorothy, of New England, spinster. Administration to
    sister and next of kin Elizabeth, wife of Henry Bannister.
    (Jan. 1684).
Elsey, Nicholas, of Merstham, Surrey. (Brother Nicholas *(sic)*
    in New England). Probate to Michael Anscombe. (June 1649).
    Sh.
Endicott, John, of Salem, New England. Probate to relict Anne
    Endicott. (Mar. 1695). Wa.
Ennis, Anne - see Clymer.
Ensigne, Thomas, of Cranbrooke, Kent. (Father Thomas Ensigne
    and brothers and sisters in New England). Probate to cousin
    John Austen. (Mar. 1658). Sh.
Enton, John, of Virginia. Administration with will to John
    Smith; no executor having been named. (Jan. 1691).
Epes, Francis the elder, of Virginia. Administration to Micajah
    Perry, attorney for son Francis Epes during his absence.
    (Oct. 1688).
Evans, Anne, of St. Bartholomew, London, who died in Virginia
    or at sea, spinster. Administration to cousin and next of
    kin Norton Westrow. (June 1681).
Evans, Laurence, of St. Benet Finck, (who died overseas with
    goods in Virginia). Administration to principal creditor
    Humphrey Streete; relict Rebecca Evans renouncing. (Sept.
    1642). Revoked on his death and granted to relict Rebecca
    Evans. (Aug. 1645).
Evans, Richard, of Virginia. Administration to relict Sarah
    Evans. (Nov. 1673).
Everigin, Catherine, of the island of Virginia, spinster.
    Administration to brother William Everigin by his solemn
    affirmation. (Nov. 1698).
Ewen(s), William, of Greenwich, Kent, mariner. (Lands in
    Virginia). Probate to relict Mary Ewens with similar powers
    reserved to daughter Mary Ewens, Thomas Stevens and Arnold
    Browne. (Aug. 1650). Sh.Wi.
Eyres, Richard, of Bermondsey, Surrey. (Bequest to Sarah
    Clapham of Virginia). Probate to relict Alice Eyres. (Feb.
    1648). Wi.

Fabian, Edmund, of Holborn, Middlesex. (Son Simon Fabian in
    Virginia). Probate to son Simon Fabian, Theophilus Smith
    and Christopher Pitt. (Aug. 1668). Wi.
Fanning, Robert, of Barking, London. (Kinsman John Fanning in
    Virginia). Probate to John Burges. (July 1672). Wi.
Fargusion, Robert, of ship *Falkland*, (of Kenton, Northumberland,
    who died in New England). Probate to George Wallis. (Feb.
    1698).
Farley, Susanna, of St. Stephen, Coleman Street, London, widow.
    (Daughter Susanna, wife of Charles Gregory of Virginia).
    Probate to John Shippey. (Apr. 1656). Wi.
Farmer, Richard, of Virginia, who died on ship *Quaker Ketch* at
    sea, bachelor. Administration to principal creditor Daniel
    Porter. (May 1689).
Farvacks, Daniel, of St. Giles Cripplegate, London, widower.
    (Credits in Virginia). Administration to son John Farvacks.
    (Oct. 1669).
Fary, Joseph, of Maryland who died on ship *James* at Virginia.
    Probate to mother Mary Fary, widow. (Nov. 1695).
Fassaker, Richard, of Stafford Co., Virginia, who died on ship
    Rappahannock Merchant at sea. Limited administration with
    will to Samuel Phillipps. (July 1676). Wi.
Fawconer, Francis, of Kingsclere, Hempshire. (Brother Edward
    Fawconer in New England). Probate to Matthew Webber. (May
    1663). Wa.
Fawne, Luke, of St. Augustine, London. (Kinswoman Elizabeth
    Clement of New England, daughter of brother John Fawne).
    Probate to John Cresset with similar powers reserved to
    John Macock. (Mar. 1666). Wa.
Fawne, Thomas, who died abroad. (Goods in Virginia). Probate
    to John Young with similar powers reserved to John Stone.
    (Aug. 1652). Sh.Wa.Wi.
Fellgate, Tobias, of Westover, Virginia. Probate to relict
    Sarah Fellgate. (Apr. 1635). Sh.Wa.
Fellowes, William, of St. Martin Vintry, London, who died in
    Virginia. Administration to son William Fellowes. (Apr.
    1682).
Fenn, Benjamin, of New England, who died at Milford, Connecticut.
    Probate to relict Susan Fenn. (Feb. 1675). Wa.
Fenn, Robert, of Wapping, Middlesex, mariner, (wife of New
    England). Probate to Thomas Bell and Mary Fenn. (Jan. 1656).
    Wa.
Fenninge, William, of St. Botolph Aldgate, London, (bound to
    Virginia). Probate to relict Margaret Fenninge. (July 1623).
    Wa.
Fenwick, George, of Worminghurst, Sussex. (Lands in New England).
    Probate to daughter Elizabeth Fenwick. (Apr. 1657). Wa.
Ferne, John, of London. (Lands in Virginia). Probate to son
    Daniel Ferne. (Jan. 1620). Sh.Wa.
Ferne, John, of ship *Catherine* who died at Virginia, bachelor.
    Administration to Anne Allen, relict of principal creditor
    John Allen deceased. (Mar. 1680).
Fielding, Ambrose, of Virginia. Probate to Edward Fielding with
    similar powers reserved to other named executors. (July 1675).
Filbrigg, Robert, of St. Dunstan in East, London. (Brother
    John Filbrigg in Virginia). Probate to brother William
    Filbrigg. (July 1638). Wi.
Filbrick, Robert, who died in New England. Administration to
    father Robert Filbrick. (May 1649).
Filleter, William, of Southampton. (Daughter Anne in Virginia).
    Probate to relict Anne Filleter. (Feb. 1659). Wi.

Filmer, Samuel, of East Sutton, Kent, but formerly of Virginia,
who died at Westminster, Middlesex. (Cousin Frances, wife
of Samuel Stephens in Virginia). Administration with will
to Warham Horsmonden, father of relict Mary Filmer alias
Horsmonden during her absence in Virginia. (May 1670).
Revoked and granted to said Mary Filmer. (Apr. 1671).
Fish, Augustine, of Bowden, Leicestershire. (Kinsman William
Fish in New England). Probate to relict Christian Fish.
(Sept. 1647). Wa.
Fisher, John, of Virginia, widower. Administration to daughter
Mary Fisher. (Oct. 1654).
Fitzer, John, of Meriland, bachelor. Administration to father
Maurice Fitzer. (Sept. 1683).
Fitzpen alias Phippen, George, clerk. (Brother David Phippen
in New England). Probate to relict Mary Phippen. (Mar.
1652). Sh.Wa.
Fleming,John, of Water Town, New England. Administration to
children Thomas Fleming and Mary, wife of John Rathery.
(Feb. 1659).
Fletcher, William, of Stepney, Middlesex, who died on ship
Elizabeth and Mary going to Virginia. Administration to
principal creditor Eleazer Bevens. (June 1659).
Fleete, Deborah, of Westminster, Middlesex, widow. (Son Henry
Fleete in Virginia). Probate to cousin Robert Filmer with
similar powers reserved to cousin Sir Edward Filmer.
(Jan. 1652). Wi.
Flower, Daniel, of London, scissormaker. (Lands in Virginia).
Probate by decree to Richard Ellis; andministration as of
intestate granted May 1670 to Alexander Martin revoked.
(June 1670).
Fly, John, of Pischadeway, New England, who died on H.M.S.
Catherine, widower. Probate of nuncupative will to William
Tavern. (Mar. 1698).
Foissin, John, of Virginia, bachelor. Administration to cousin
Abraham Palmentier. (Dec. 1694).
Follett, John, (of Cape Henry, Virginia) who died on H.M.S.
Deptford. Probate to Richard Mills. (Jan. 1692).
Foote, Richard, of St. Dunstan in East, London. (Lands in
Virginia). Probate to relict Hester Foote; other executor
son Samuel Foote having died. (Apr. 1697).
Forby, Felix, of Norwich, hosier. (Son and daughter in Vir-
ginia). Probate to son-in-law Richard Coates and Martha
his wife. (Jan. 1661). Wi.
Fortee, Henry, of Lambeth, Surrey, who died at Virginia on
East India Company ship *Josiah*. Limited administration to
brothers Benjamin and Charles Fortee. (Nov. 1691).
Foster, Elizabeth, of Crutched Friars, London. (Widow of
Henry Foster of Virginia). Probate to mother Elizabeth
Higginson. (Mar. 1674). Wa.
Foulks, Thomas, of Princess Anne Co., Virginia. Probate to
John Vicary by decree. (Sept. & Oct. 1692). Wa.
Fownes, John, of Plymouth, Devon, merchant. (Adventurer to
Virginia or New England). Administration with will to
brother Warwick Fownes; named executor having died. (Feb.
1625). Wa.
Fox, John, of Virginia, bachelor. Administration to father
Edward Fox. (Feb. 1668).
Fox, Stephen, of ship *Fortune* who died overseas (near New
England). Administration with will to brother John Fox;
no executor having been named. (Oct. 1663). Wa.Wi.
Foxwell, George, of Virginia, bachelor. Administration to
brother and next of kin Henry Foxwell. (Aug. 1673).

Fry, Samuel, of Virginia, bachelor. Administration to mother
Anne Fry, widow. (Mar. 1656).

Fryer, Sibell, of New Sarum, Wiltshire, widow. (Bequest to
John Bennett in New England). Probate to daughters Margaret
Good and Anne Jempson. (Feb. 1636). Wa.

Fullerton, Alexander, of Maryland who died on ship *Elizabeth*,
bachelor. Administration to brother Isaac Fullerton.
(Aug. 1694).

Gadsby, Edward, of ship *Redbridge*, (of Stepney, Middlesex,
bound to Virginia). Probate to John Duffield. (Apr. 1696).
Wa.

Garrard, Anne, of Up Lambourne, Berkshire, widow. (Grandchild
Anne, wife of Thomas Hinton lately gone to Virginia).
Probate to Jane Busher. (Feb. 1635).

Garraway, Richard, of New England. Administration to relict
Anne Garraway. (July 1668).

Gault alias Galtt, James, of Stepney, Middlesex, who died on
H.M.S. *Dove's* Prize at Virginia. Probate to relict Alice
Gault. (Sept. 1697).

Gaylard, Robert, of Virginia, bachelor. Administration to
mother Mary Gaylard, widow. (Apr. 1657).

Gayny, Anne, of Virginia, widow. Administration to creditor
Edward Hurd. (Jan. 1643).

Geary, John, of Dunsley, Tring, Hertfordshire. (Lands in
Pennsylvania). Probate to Henry Geary. (Dec. 1696).

Geere, Dennis, of Saugus, Massachusetts, who died overseas.
Administration with will to Edward Moncke, maternal uncle
to daughters Elizabeth and Sarah Geere during their minority;
relict Elizabeth Geere having died. (June 1642). Sh.Wa.

Gembell, Adam, of St. Martin in Fields, Middlesex, who died in
Carolina, bachelor. Administration to brother John Gembell.
(Aug. 1696).

Gerrard, Henry, of St. Martin'Brandon, Charles City Co., Virginia. Administration with will to Micajah Perry, attorney
for sons Ferdinand and Nicholas Gerrard in Virginia; no
executor having been named. (Mar. 1693). Wi.

Gibbons, Margaret, of New England who died at Plymouth, Devon.
Administration to daughter Jerusha, wife of Captain Thomas
Rea. (Feb. 1657).

Gibbs, Philip, of Bristol, (bound for Virginia). Administration
with will to Anthony Marshall; named executor Philip Marshall
having died. (Oct. 1674). Wa.

Gibbs, Richard, of St. Dunstan in West, London, who died at New
York in West Indies. Administration to relict Elizabeth,
now wife of Peter Ludgar. (Oct. 1683).

Gibson, John, of ship *Assurance* who died at James River, Virginia. Probate to Edward Kirby. (Oct. 1692).

Gibson, William, of St. Edmund the King, London. (Goods in New
Jersey and Pennsylvania). Administration with will to Jane
Barnes, guardian of children John, William and Patience
Gibson during their minority; relict Elizabeth Gibson
renouncing. (Jan. 1685).

23

Gill, William, of Stepney, Middlesex, who died in Virginia,
    widower. Administration to principal creditor John Booty.
    (July 1668).
Gilliard, Andrew, of ship *King of Poland* who died at Virginia,
    bachelor. Administration to cousin german and next of kin
    John Pulling. (Apr. 1656).
Gittings, Adam, of Virginia, bachelor. Administration to
    sister Sarah Smith alias Gittings in the absence overseas
    of mother Elizabeth Gittings. (Sept. 1670).
Glanvell, William, of Virginia. Administration to relict Alice
    Glanvell. (Sept. 1668).
Glocester alias Warkman, Mark, of St. Mary Magdalen, London.
    (Brother Robert in Virginia). Probate to relict Elizabeth
    Glocester alias Warkman. (Apr. 1670). Wi.
Glover, Jose, of London who died overseas. (Lands in New
    England). Probate to Richard Davies with similar powers
    reserved to John Harris. (Dec. 1638). Wa.
Glover, Mary, of St. Olave, Silver Street, London, widow.
    Daughter Bennett Glover of Virginia). Probate to John
    Watson. (July 1661). Wa.
Glover, Nicholas, who died in Virginia, bachelor. Administra-
    tion to nephew by a sister John Carter. (Aug. 1612).
Glover, Richard, of Virginia, who died at sea on ship *Maryland*,
    widower. Administration to brother Charles Glover. (Aug.
    1684). Revoked on his death and granted to nephew Charles
    Glover. (Nov. 1684).
Goddard, Edmund, of Virginia, bachelor. Probate to sister
    Hannah Sheffield alias Goddard. (Dec. 1681).
Goddard, Thomas, of Talbott Co., Maryland. Administration to
    relict Grace Brockney alias Goddard. (Nov. 1687).
Godwyn, Mary, of Lyme Regis, Dorset, widow. (Brother William
    Hill in New England). Probate to John Farrant, Robert
    Burridge and William Courtney. (June 1665). Wa.
Goldstone, Edward, of Limehouse, Stepney, Middlesex, mariner.
    (Goods in Virginia). Probate to relict Sarah Goldstone and
    Rev. Malachi Harris. (July 1663). Wi.
Golledge, Thomas, of Chichester, Sussex. (Provides for children
    to be transported to New England). Probate to relict Mary
    College *(sic)*. (June 1648). Wa.
Gondry, William, of London who died overseas, (bound for Virginia).
    Probate to Thomas Palmer. (Apr. 1638). Double probate to
    mother Anne Preston. (July 1638). Sh.Wi.(in the latter
    listed under *Goudrey*).
Good, Benjamin, of Virginia, bachelor. Administration to brother
    John Good. (Aug. 1672).
Goode, Marmaduke, of Upton, Berkshire, clerk. (Brother John
    Goode in Virginia). Probate to Samuel and Mary Goode.
    (Feb. 1678). Wa,
Goodall, Elizabeth, of New England. Administration to son James
    Goodall. (June 1651).
Goodfellowe, Alin, of St. Laurence Jewry, London, who died in
    Virginia. Probate to brother Christopher Goodfellowe.
    (May 1638). Sh.Wi.
Goodman, William, of ship *Honor's Desire* who died in Virginia,
    bachelor. Administration to principal creditor Thomas Batson.
    (July 1663).
Gorges, John, of St. Margaret, Westminster, Middlesex. (Lands
    in Maine, New England). Probate to Ferdinando Gorges.
    (June 1657). Sh.
Gosnold, Robert, of Earl Soham, Suffolk. (Grandchild Anthony
    Gosnold in Virginia). Probate to son Anthony Gosnold with
    similar powers reserved to Thomas Cornewallis. (Nov. 1615). Wi.

Gough, Charles, of Maryland, widower. Administration to
  Stephen Noguier, guardian of infant son Thomas Gough.
  (July 1699). Further grant November 1700.
Gould, Judith, of Watford, Hertfordshire, widow. (Son Nathan
  in New England). Probate to children Abel, Lydia and
  Elizabeth Gould. (Sept. 1650). Wa.
Gradwell, Jacob, who died on ship *Preston* (at Cooper River,
  South Carolina). Probate to Edward Hoole. (Oct. 1699).
  See NGSQ 64/139.
Granger, Robert, of Maryland. Administration to cousins and
  next of kin William Granger and Elizabeth Benskin. (Nov.
  1690).
Grant, Jasper, of Stepney, Middlesex, who died in Virginia.
  Administration to principal creditor Edmund Bugden; relict
  Judith Grant renouncing. (Feb. 1663).
Grave, Anne, of St. Botolph Aldgate, London, widow. (Kinsmen
  George Grave of Hartford, Connecticut, and John Grave of
  New Haven, New England). Probate to William Kiffin; James
  Orbell renouncing. (Mar. 1677). Revoked on death of William
  Kiffin and administration granted to his executors Joseph and
  Jonathan Hardey. (Oct. 1688).
Grave, John, of Virginia. Administration with will to nephew
  by a sister Walter Potter during absence of executor John
  Murrey. (Sept. 1692). Sh.
Gray, Grace, of Symondsbury, Dorset, widow. Administration to
  daughter Grace, wife of John Kemble now in Virginia. (Mar.
  1695).
Grey, Henry, of St. Botolph Aldgate, London, who died in Virginia.
  Administration with will to principal creditor Richard Banckes;
  relict Elizabeth Kerby alias Grey renouncing. (June 1675).
Grey, William, of London who died at Hackney, Middlesex. (Brother
  John Grey in New England). Probate to relict Susan Grey.
  (Nov. 1663). Wa.
Greene, Edward, of Bristol who died in Virginia. Probate to
  brother Robert Greene. (Aug. 1698). Wa.
Green, John, of Petsoe, Gloucester Co., Virginia. Probate to
  relict Anne Green. (Jan. 1694). Wa.
Greene, Peter, of ship *Charles* who died in Virginia. Admini-
  stration to Mary, wife of brother Edward Greene. (July 1678).
Greene, Robert, of Stepney, Middlesex. (Bequest to Thomas
  Reynolds in Virginia). Probate to Thomas Snow. (Sept. 1658).
  Wa.
Greenough, William, of Boston, New England, who died abroad or
  at sea. Administration to principal creditor Benjamin Peake,
  merchant. (May 1684).
Gregory, William, of Nottingham. (Brother Henry Gregory in New
  England). Probate to son John Gregory. (Feb. 1652). Wa.
Gregson, Richard, of St. Augustine by St. Paul, London. (Kinsman
  Thomas Gregson in New England). Probate to son Nicholas
  Gregson. (Aug. 1640). Wa.
Grendon, Thomas, of Westover, Charles City Co., Virginia.
  Limited probate to Arthur North. (Apr. 1685). Sh.Wa.
Grey - see Gray.
Gribb, John, of Stepney, Middlesex, who died at Virginia.
  Administration to principal creditor John Sackell; relict
  Susan Gribb renouncing. (June 1698).
Griffin, David, of St. Michael Bassishaw, London. (Brother
  Samuel Griffin in Virginia). Probate to John Hobbs. (Dec.
  1679). Wa.
Griffin, Elizabeth, of Virginia, widow. Administration to niece
  by a sister and next of kin Lidya, wife of Thomas Tonstall.
  (Nov. 1689). Wa. Inventory PROB4/1035.

Griffyn, Joanna, of Virginia. Probate to George Griffyn.
(Apr. 1661). Wa.
Griffin, Thomas, of ship *Hope* who died at Virginia, widower.
Probate to Solomon Amos. (July 1697).
Griggs, Michael, (of Lancaster Co., Virginia), late of St.
Botolph Aldgate, London, who died at St. Matthew, Friday
Street, London. Probate to relict Anne, now wife of Richard
Bray. (Sept. 1688). Wa.
Grimditch, Thomas, of New York. Administration to relict
Eshew Grimditch. (Mar. 1684).
Groome, John, of Strood, Kent. (Goods in New England).
Probate to relict ---ce Groome. (June 1658). Sh.
Groome, Nicholas, who died in Virginia. Probate to ----- Wall
and Henry Groome. (Apr. 1652). Sh.
Groome, Thomas, of ship *Falkland* in H.M. service who died in
New England. Administration to principal creditrix Anne,
wife of John Severne. (Apr. 1698).
Gunnell, George, of Shoreditch, Middlesex, who died in Virginia.
Administration to relict Rebecca Gunnell. (July 1674).
Guy, Edward, of Appleby, Westmoreland, who died in Philadelphia.
Administration to son John Guy. (Apr. 1698).
Guy, Frances, of St. Botolph Bishopsgate, Middlesex, widow.
(Brother William Clutterbuck in New England). Probate to
John Heyth MD. (Aug 1680). Wa.
Guy, William, of St. Mildred, Broad Street, London. (Cousin
John Gate in Virginia). Probate to William Allen and
Anthony Field. (Nov. 1665). Wi.
Gwin, John, of James City, Virginia. Administration with will
to Thomas Starke, attorney for executor Henry Jenkins in
Virginia. (Nov. 1684). Wi.

Hacker, John, of Limehouse, Stepney, Middlesex. (Lands in
Virginia). Probate to relict Elizabeth Hacker. (June 1654).
Wa.
Hacker, John, of Bermondsey, Surrey, who died in Virginia.
Administration to relict Joyce Hacker. (Nov. 1690).
Haddocke, William, of Virginia who died overseas. Probate to
brother Richard Haddocke. (Aug. 1649). Sh.Wa.
Hainsworth, Francis, of St. Sepulchre, London. (Goods in
Virginia). Administration with will to John White; no
executor having been named. (Feb. 1657). Wa.Wi.
Hailes, Elizabeth, of Shadwell, Stepney, Middlesex. (Cousin
William Foster in New England). Probate to Thomas Parker
and William Bugby. (Sept. 1664). Wa.
Hales, Sarah, of New England. Administration to Walter Hales,
attorney for husband Richard Hales in New England. (May
1696).
Halford, John, of St. Catherine Creechurch, London, bachelor,
who died at Virginia. Administration to sister Alice
Crisdell; previous grant of May 1690 to sister Dorothy
Benson now revoked because of her death. (Apr. & May 1693).
Hall, Charles, who died at Virginia, bachelor. Probate to
Peter Martell. (June 1699).

Hall, Richard, of London who died in Virginia, widower. Administration to son Richard Hall. (Jan. 1668).

Hall, Thomas, of St. Katherine by Tower, London. (Brother John Hall in New England). Probate to relict Judith Hall. (May 1663). Wa.NGSQ 64/137.

Hallett, Lancelott, of Maryland on River Sarifax in Virginia, bachelor. Administration to brother Richard Hallett. (July 1671).

Halsey, Esau, of Suffolk, New England, bachelor. Administration to John Bynne during absence overseas of brother William Halsey. (Sept. 1677).

Halsted, Abraham, of Rotterdam. (Sister in New England). Probate to relict Dorcas Whitman alias Halsted with similar powers reserved to William Scapes. (May 1651). Sh.Wa.

Hanbury, Edward, of Old Brentford, Ealing, Middlesex. (Son Peter in New England). Probate to relict Mary Hanbury. (Apr. 1647). Wa.

Hance, Rawleigh, of Shadwell, Middlesex, who died in Virginia, bachelor. Administration to brother Edward Wren alias Hance. (Oct. 1673).

Handford, John, of Ludlow, Shropshire. (Kinsman Tobias Handford in Virginia). Probate to relict Elinor Handford; Sir Walter Williams and Sir John Winford renouncing. (Jan. 1670). Wi.

Handford, Tobias, formerly of Virginia who died at St. George, Botolph Lane, London. Probate to Elizabeth and John Handford and William Smith. (Dec. 1677). Wi.

Hannyford, Edward, of Virginia. Administration to relict Marchebell Hannyford. (June 1656).

Hardich, William, of Nominy, Westmoreland Co., Virginia, who died in Bristol. Probate to Thomas Burgis and Richard Winston. (Jan. 1669). Wi.

Harmer, Charles, of Virginia. Administration to creditor Richard Roch. (July 1639).

Harrendon, Tristian, of New England, bachelor. Administration to cousin and next of kin Philip White. (Sept. 1681).

Harris, George, of Westover, Charles Co., Virginia. Administration with nuncupative will to relict Sarah Greendon alias Harris; no executor having been named. (Aug. 1674). Wi.

Harris, John, of Hillmarton, Wiltshire. (Lands in Pennsylvania). Probate to relict Jane Harris and son Samuel Harris. (June 1693).

Harris alias Crumpe, Mary (*Jane* in margin), of Virginia. Administration to daughter Martha, wife of John Jennings. (June 1656).

Harris, Priscilla, of Northam, Devon, spinster. (Sister Agnes in New England). Probate to brother Richard Harris. (Sept. 1651). Sh.Wa.

Harris, Stephen, of Norham, Devon Co., Virginia or Maryland. Administration to relict Margaret Harris. (Aug. 1699).

Harrison, Henrick, of ship *Barnardiston* who died in Virginia. Probate to Anne Thompson alias Holliday. (Mar. 1694).

Harrison, Margaret, of Battersea, Surrey, widow. (Bequest to Alice Andrewes in New England). Probate to son Thomas Andrewes. (Mar. 1642). Wa.

Harrison, Nicholas, of Virginia who died at St. Sepulchre, London, bachelor. Administration with will to mother Dorothy Harrison; no executor having been named. (Sept. 1653). Sh.Wa.Wi.

Harrison, Thomas, of Rotherhithe, Surrey, who died in New England, bachelor. Administration to father Edmund Harrison. (Dec. 1669).

Hartwell, Henry, (of Virginia) who died at Stepney, Middlesex.
Probate to Micajah and Richard Perry. (Aug. 1699). Wa.

Harvey, Sir John, of London, bachelor, who died overseas (with
interests in Virginia). Administration with will to Alice
Dixon, relict and administratrix of Thomas Dixon. (July
1650). Sh.

Harvey, Robert, of New England, bachelor. Administration to
cousin german and next of kin Margaret Dorrell, wife of
John Dorrell, "for that the estate was in danger of being
left in regard hee the said John Dorrell being gone a
voyage to the Straights." (May 1655).

Harwood, Andrew, of Virginia. Administration to Edmond Pike,
guardian of children Sarah, Margaret and James Harwood
during their minority. (Aug. 1659).

Harwood, Arthur, of St. Peter ad Vincula, London, (formerly
of Virginia), who died overseas. Probate to Alexander
Harwood. (Dec. 1642). Sh.Wi.

Harwood, Elizabeth, of Bethnal Green, Middlesex, widow.
(Brother Hezekiah Usher of New England). Probate to James
Harwood. (Apr. 1687). Wa.

Harwood, John, of St. Leonard, Shoreditch, Middlesex. (Brother
Thomas Harwood, daughter Elizabeth Sedgwick and other kin in
New England). Probate to relict Elizabeth Harwood. (June
1685). Wa.

Haswell, John, of Stepney, Middlesex, who died at Virginia.
Administration to relict Sarah Haswell. (July 1682).

Hatton, John, of Virginia. Probate to brother Thomas Hatton;
other executor Robert Lewellin having died. (July 1663).

Haviland, Matthew, of Shoreditch, Middlesex, clerk. (Sister
Jane, wife of William Torry of New England). Probate to
relict Constance Haviland. (Feb. 1671). Wa.

Hawker, George, of St. Martin Ludgate, London. (Brother Edward
Hawker in Virginia). Probate to relict Martha Hawker.
(Jan. 1658). Sh.Wi.

Hawker, Humphrey, of St. Mary le Bow, London. (Daughter Dorothy
in Virginia). Probate to John Oresbie with similar powers
reserved to Henry Hodges. (Nov. 1647). Wi.

Hawkins, Anne, of Virginia, spinster. Administration to brother
Matthew Hawkins. (July 1654).

Hawkins, William, of Kingston on Thames, Surrey, who died in New
England. Probate to sister Rachel Wade alias Sudell, wife of
Christopher Wade, with similar powers reserved to Frances
Blanch. (July 1686). Further grant April 1702.

Hawley, Jeremiah, of Maryland near Virginia. Administration to
principal creditor Thomas Cornwallis. (Jan. 1651).

Hay, James, of Cloughton near Scarborough, Yorkshire, who died
in Virginia. Administration to relict Priscilla Hay. (Oct.
1678).

Heyes, Hugh, of Presbury, Cheshire. (Cousin William Stone in
Virginia). Probate to brother-in-law Benjamin Bannester.
(May 1637). Wi.

Haighes, John, who died at Virginia, bachelor. Administration
to brother Edward Haighes. (Jan. 1628).

Hayes, Joseph, of Virginia. Probate by decree to Anne Hayes
with similar powers reserved to son William Hayes. (June
1678). Wi.

Hayward, John, of Rappahannock River, Virginia, bachelor.
Administration to mother Charity Britton alias Hayward.
(Oct. 1698).

Hayward, Thomas, (of Beverley, New York) who died on H.M.S.
Royal William. Probate to Margaret Eldridge. (Sept. 1694).

Hayward, Thomas, of Rappahannock River, Virginia, who died on
  ship *William and Mary* at sea. Administration to relict
  Charity, now wife of John Britton. (Oct. 1698).
Hearne - see Herne.
Heathcote, Nathaniel, of Anne Arundell Co., Maryland. Admini-
  stration to grandson Samuel Heathcote. (July 1682).
Henderson, Henry, (of York River, Virginia), who died at
  Clerkenwell, Middlesex. Probate to Richard Stone. (Nov.
  1674). Wi.
Herne, Sir Nathaniel, alderman of London. (Niece Whitlock in
  Virginia). Probate to Sir John Fredericke, Joseph Herne,
  William Wheatley and John Banckes. (Aug. 1679). Revoked
  and administration granted to son Nathaniel Herne; John
  Banckes not appearing and the other executors having died.
  (Dec. 1694). Wi.
Heyrne alias Iron, Nicholas, who died on ship *James Towne*
  coming from Virginia. Administration to brother
  William Heyrne alias Iron. (Dec. 1659).
Hearne, Peter, of Carolina, who died in H.M.S. *Monmouth*.
  Administration to relict Joan Hearne. (Jan. 1696).
Herring, Arthur, of Maryland. Administration to sister Mary
  Herring. (Sept. 1691).
Hewet, Sir Thomas, of St. Martin in Fields, Middlesex, (of
  Old Jewry, London, adventurer in Virginia). Probate to
  brother Sir William Hewett. (Feb. 1624). Wi.
Hey, Eleanor, of East Greenwich, Kent. Administration to John
  Grant of East Greenwich, glover, attorney for husband James
  Hey now at (New) England. (Apr. 1695).
Heyes - see Hayes.
Heyrne - see Herne.
Heywood, Richard, of Stepney, Middlesex, who died at Virginia.
  Administration to John Hill principal creditor and guardian
  of children Richard, Elizabeth and Rebecca Heywood; relict
  Elizabeth Heywood renouncing. (Aug. 1695).
Hickman, William, of St. Swithin, London. (Kinsman Joseph
  Hickman in Virginia). Probate to relict Margaret Hickman.
  (Sept. 1672). Wa.
Higginson, Humphrey, of Ratcliffe, Stepney, Middlesex. (Brother
  Christopher Higginson in Virginia). Probate to relict
  Elizabeth Higginson. (Mar. 1666). Wa.
Highlord, Katherine, of St. Stephen, Coleman Street, London,
  widow. (Cousins Robert and Richard Wilson in Virginia).
  Probate to Robert Wilson. (July 1648). Wa.
Hill, John, of St. Olave, Hart Street, London, merchant.
  (Brother Valentine Hill of New England). Probate to relict
  Sarah Hill. (Feb. 1688). Wa.
Hill, Richard, of Cookham, Berkshire, (bound for New England),
  who died overseas, bachelor. Probate to Nicholas Greene.
  (Sept. 1635).
Hill, Samuel, of Virginia, bachelor. Probate to father Edward
  Hill. (Aug. 1695).
Hilson, George, master of ship *Friends Increase* who died at
  Virginia. Administration to principal creditor Anthony
  Phillips; relict Anne Hilson renouncing. (May 1679).
Hilton, Nowell, of Charles Town, Middlesex Co., New England,
  mariner. Administration with will to Nathaniel Cutler; no
  executor having been named. (Sept. 1689). Wa.
Hind, William, of Virginia, widower. Administration to son
  William Hind. (Mar. 1673).
Hitch, Mildred, of St. John Evangelist, London, widow. (Kins-
  woman Mary Johnson formerly Hazard of New England). Probate
  to Robert Hitch. (Mar. 1658). Sh.Wa.

Hitchins, Samuel, of All Hallows, Barking, London. (Nephews
  Daniel and Joseph Hitchins in New England). Probate to
  Daniel Morse and Nicholas Morse; Robert Hitchins renouncing.
  (Dec. 1679). Sh.
Hobbs, Joseph, of Crewkerne, Somerset, who died in New England,
  bachelor. Administration to sister Margaret Hobbs. (June
  1697).
Hobbs, Dr. Thomas, of St. Clement Danes, Middlesex. (Sister
  Elizabeth, wife of Francis Weekes of Middlesex Co., Virginia).
  Probate to Sir John Hawles, John Lilly and relict Catherine
  Hobbs, with similar powers reserved to Sir John Somers.
  (Oct. 1698). See NGSQ 62/38.
Hodges, Peter, of East West Jersey who died at Bermondsey,
  Surrey. Probate to Elizabeth Willis. (Dec. 1697). Wa.
Holcombe, John, of Virginia, bachelor. Administration to
  principal creditor John Wilcox. (May 1670).
Holcroft, George, of Virginia, bachelor. Administration to
  father Michael Holcroft. (Dec. 1666).
Holding, Peter, of ship *Resolution*, widower, who died in New
  England. Administration to daughter Elizabeth Holding.
  (Dec. 1693).
Holland, Joseph, citizen and clothworker of London. (Daughter
  Elizabeth, wife of Richard Bessy in Virginia; son Nathaniel
  Holland in New England; son Samuel Holland in Virginia).
  Probate to John White. (Jan. 1658). Wa.
Holland, Joshua, of Shadwell, Middlesex. (Daughter Elizabeth
  in Pennsylvania). Probate to son Thanks Holland with similar
  powers reserved to Frances Jackson. (May 1690).
Hollister, George, of Boston, New England, who died on H.M.
  fireship *Hawk*, bachelor. Administration to heir Prospero
  Winchester of Pandon Magna. (Dec. 1693).
Holmes, William, who died overseas. (Bequest to enable his two
  children to go to Virginia). Probate to nephews Oliver
  Holmes and Richard Graby. (Feb. 1649). Sh.
Holton, John, of H.M.S. *Greenwich* who died at Maryland, bachelor.
  Administration to father Thomas Holton. (July 1697).
Honywood, John, who died in America, bachelor. Probate to Thomas
  Denne. (Jan. 1639). Sh.
Hooker, Col. Edward, of St. Mary at Hill, London. (Sister
  Mary Hooker in New England). Probate to son Cornelius Hooker;
  relict Elizabeth Hooker renouncing. (July 1651).
Hooker, John, of Marefield, Leicestershire. (Cousin Samuel
  Hooker in New England). Probate to William Jennings. (Nov.
  1655). Wa.
Hooker, Mary, of Island of Virginia, spinster. Administration
  to cousin and next of kin Oliver Gregory. (Oct. 1682).
Hooker, Peter, (bound to Virginia), who died overseas, bachelor.
  Probate to brother Edward Hooker. (Nov. 1639). Sh.Wi.
Hooker, Ralph, (of Barbados), who died overseas. (Cousin Richard
  Bennett of New England). Probate to John Hooker. (May 1665).
  Wa.
Hopkins, Edward, of St. Olave, Hart Street, London. (Goods in
  New England). Probate to nephew Henry Dalley. (Apr. 1657).
  Sh.
Hopkins, Henry, of London. (Goods in New England). Probate to
  nephew Henry Dalley. (Apr. 1657). Wa.
Hopkinson, Daniel, who died overseas. (Goods in Virginia).
  Probate to brother Joseph Clifton. (Apr. 1637). Sh.Wi.
Horwood, Joel, (of Boston), of H.M.S. *Sheerness*. Probate to
  brother Henry Horwood. (Aug. 1697).
Hoskins, Mary, of Richmond, Surrey, widow. (Brother John Githins
  in Maryland). Probate to brother William Githins. (Feb.
  1678). Wa.

Hough, Francis, of St. Peter le Poor, London. (Son William
Hough to be sent to Virginia). Administration with will to
Anne Cooke, grandmother of children William, John, Jane and
Ann Hough during their minority. (July 1648). Revoked on
her death and granted to children John Hough, Jane Andrewes
and Anne Tirrick, now come of age. (Sept. 1667). Wi.
Houghton, Robert, of St. Olave, Southwark, Surrey. (Sister
Mary, wife of Francis Norton of New England). Probate to
relict Mary Houghton. (Jan. 1653). Wa.
Howe, Elizabeth, of St. Giles, Cripplegate, London, widow.
(Son-in-law Edward Hill of Virginia). Probate to Edward
Hill and Sarah Alcorne. (May. 1677). Wi.
Howell, Edward, of St. Mary Woolnoth, London, who died at
Carolina. Administration to principal creditor Anthony
Church; relict Mary Howell renouncing. (Oct. 1692).
Howes, William, of Virginia. Administration to son Richard
Howes. (May 1694).
Howett, John, of Elizabeth City, Virginia. Probate to Thomas
Howett. (July 1659). Wi.
Hubbard, Thomas, of Virginia, bachelor. Administration to
brother Edward Hubbard. (Sept. 1697).
Huckstep, Samuel, (of King and Queen Co., Virginia) and Ewhurst,
Sussex. Probate to relict Jane Huckstep. (Jan. 1696).
Huggins, Robert, of Carolina, bachelor. Probate to William
Peasley. (Nov. 1677).
Humfreys, John, of Honiton, Devon, who died in Virginia, widower.
Administration to brother Henry Humfreys. (Sept. 1656).
Hunlocke, Martha, of Clapham, Surrey, widow. (Son Edward
Hunlocke in New England). Probate to William Hardcastle.
(Jan 1691). Wa.
Hunt, John, of Virginia. Administration to relict Thomasine
Hunt. (Oct. 1669).
Hunt, Thomas, of Chalfont St. Giles, Buckinghamshire, who died
at Carolina. Probate to brother Andrew Hunt; named execu-
tors renouncing. (Aug. 1699).
Hutchinson, Abraham, of Virginia, bachelor. Administration to
brother John Hutchinson. (May 1687).
Hutchinson, Richard, citizen and ironmonger of London and of
Hertford. (Lands in New England). Probate to Edward
Hutchinson with similar powers reserved to other executors.
(Apr. 1670). Wa.
Hutchinson, Robert, of Virginia. Administration to sister Jane
Daberry. (July 1650).
Hyde, Sir Henry, of London.¯ (Lands in Virginia). Probate to
brothers Thomas Hyde, doctor of laws, and James Hyde, MD.
(June 1660). Sh.Wi.

Indian, Thomas, of Bristol Township, New England, who died on
H.M.S. *Dolphin* at Barbados, bachelor. Administration to
principal creditor Thomas Newton. (Apr. 1695).
Ingoldsby, Mary - see Langhorne.
Ingram, Joseph, (bound for Virginia) who died overseas. Probate
to father Robert Ingram. (Sept. 1653). Sh.Wi.

Irby, Walter, of Ackee Mack, Northampton Co., Virginia, who
died overseas. Probate to mother Olive Irby alias Cooper,
widow. (July 1652). Sh.Wi.
Ireland, John, of Boston, New England, who died at sea.
Administration to John Lane, attorney for relict Mary Ireland
in New England. (Jan. 1699).
Irish, Zachary, of Windsor, Berkshire. (Brother Edward Newman
in Virginia). Probate to John Weekes and Richard Newman.
(July 1672). Wa.
Iron, Nicholas - see Herne.
Ironmonger, Martha - see Jones.
Ironmonger, Corderoy, of Virginia, bachelor. Administration to
sister Elizabeth Everndon alias Ironmonger, wife of Anthony
Everndon. (Nov. 1681).
Isham, Henry, of Virginia. Probate to William Randolph.
(June 1680). Wa.Wi.
Isham, Thomas, of Middle Temple, London. (Cousin Henry Isham
of Virginia). Probate to Francis Drake. (July 1676). Wi.
Ive, John, of Boston, New England. Administration to Benjamin
Stow, father of relict Sarah Ive until she is 21. (Oct. 1698).

Jackson, Samuel, of Boston, Lincolnshire. (Sister Mary Wood-
ward in Boston, New England). Administration with will to
brother Nathaniel Jackson; no executor having been named.
(Nov. 1646). Wa.
Jackson, Samuel, (of New England), who died on H.M.S. *Windsor
Castle*. Probate to Anthony Dowrich. (Feb. 1693). Wa.
Jacob, William, of Deptford, Kent, who died in Virginia,
bachelor. Administration to mother Anne Jacob. (Apr.1682).
Jadwyn, Thomas, of St. Michael, Paternoster Row, London.
(Lands in Virginia). Probate to relict Elizabeth Jadwyn.
(Mar. 1628). Wa.
James, Edward, of Virginia. Administration to sisters Margery,
wife of Christopher Price, Ellinor, wife of John Richardson,
and Mary James. (June 1659).
Janson, Thomazine, of St. Dunstan in West, London, widow.
(Kinswomen Judith Tower and Elizabeth Winthrop in New
England). Probate to Thomas Essington with similar powers
reserved to Thomas Oldfield. (Feb. 1659). Wa.
Jarvis, Thomas, of St. Olave, Old Jewry, London, (and late of
Virginia). Probate to relict Elizabeth Jarvis, Edmund
Foster and George Richards. (Apr. 1684).
Jeffries, David, of Taunton, Somerset. (Son David Jeffries
of New England). Probate to relict Dorothy Jeffries and
daughters Sarah and Hester Jeffries. (Jan. 1691). Wa.
Jeffreys, Herbert, (Governor of Virginia), who died in Virginia.
Administration to Bartholomew Price, attorney for relict
Susanna Jeffreys and son John Jeffreys. (May 1679) See
NGSQ 66/118.
Jeffs, Charles, of ship *St. John* who died at Virginia, bachelor.
Administration to mother Mary Jeffs, widow. (Apr. 1694).
Jenny, John, of St. Mary at Hill, London, who died in Virginia,
bachelor. Administration to brother Samuel Jenny. (Aug.
1676). Further grant July 1734.

Jesson, James, of St. Andrew Undershaft, London. (Lands in
New England). Administration with will to relict Mary Jesson;
executor Richard Lloyd having died and surviving executor
George Scott renouncing. (Aug. 1686). Wa.
Joddrell, William, of H.M.S. *Dunbarton* who died at Virginia,
bachelor. Administration to principal creditor Thomas
Collin. (Apr. 1692).
Johnson, Daniel, of Lynn, New England, who died at St. Thomas
Hospital, Southwark, Surrey, from H.M.S. *Advice*. Probate
to Patrick Hayes. (Apr. 1696).
Johnson, John, of ship *Concordat* who died at Virginia, bachelor.
Probate to Jane Cheney with similar powers reserved to
Robert Cheney. (July 1682).
Johnson, John, of Virginia, bachelor. Administration to Dorcas,
wife of principal creditor Gerard Dobson during his absence.
"Pauper." (July & Oct. 1688).
Johnson, Luke, of Virginia. Probate to John Turton and James
Cary. (Aug. 1659). Sh.Sm.Wi.
Johnson, Nicholas, of Shadwell, Middlesex, who died in Virginia.
Administration to principal creditor Roger Stackhouse; relict
Emma Johnson renouncing. (Apr. 1663).
Johnson, Peter, of ship *Anne* who died at Virginia, bachelor.
Probate to Gabriel Whitehorne. (Aug. 1693).
Johnson alias Duncombe, Susanna, of Virginia. Administration
to Gawen Corbin, attorney for husband Col. Richard Johnson
in Virginia. (Oct. 1694).
Jones, Anne, of St. Clement Danes, Middlesex. (Son Thomas
Daniell in Virginia). Probate to said Thomas Daniell.
(Feb. 1678). Wa.
Jones, Jane - see Vaughan.
Jones, Josias, of Greenwich, Kent, who died at Virginia.
Administration to relict Hannah Jones. (Sept. 1686).
Jones alias Ironmonger, Martha, wife of John Jones of Virginia.
Administration to Elizabeth Evernden alias Ironmonger, wife
of Anthony Evernden, maternal aunt of son John Jones during
his absence. (Nov. 1681).
Jones, Owen, of H.M.S. *Richmond* who died at New York. Limited
probate to George Farewell, attorney for relict Elizabeth
Jones. (Oct. 1698).
Jones, Richard, of St. Clement Eastcheap, London, who died at
Virginia. Administration to relict Frances Williams alias
Jones. (June 1659).
Jones, Samuel, of ship *Warspight* in King's service, (and of
Gloucester, New England), who died at St. Thomas, Southwark,
Surrey. Probate to sister Susan Smith. (Oct. 1673).
Jones, Samuel, of ship *Jacob (?James)*, who died on ship *Yorke*
(bound for Virginia,) bachelor. Probate to brother John
Jones. (May 1693).
Jones, Thomas, who died in Virginia. Administration to prin-
cipal creditor Rowland Gold. (Apr. 1626).
Jones, Thomas, of H.M.S. *Pembroke* who died at Virginia. Probate
to Dyer Wade; previous grant of November 1697 to Elizabeth,
wife of Richard Jones during absence of executor now revoked.
(Oct. 1698).
Jordan, Robert, of island of Portland who died in Virginia.
Administration to relict Joanne Jordan. (Nov. 1668). New
grant November 1688. Inventory PROB4/1101.
Joy, Erasmus, of Plymouth, Devon, who died at Virginia.
Administration to relict Jane Joy. (Nov. 1682).
Joy, George, of Boston, New England. Administration to Mary,
wife and attorney of principal creditor Francis Davis during
his absence. (Oct. 1680).

Joyner, Thomas, of Stepney, Middlesex, who died at Virginia.
Administration to principal creditor Dalby Thomas; relict
Jane Joyner renouncing. (July 1675).

Juxon, Thomas, of Mortlake, Surrey. (Cousin William Juxon of
Virginia. Probate to daughter Elizabeth Juxon. (Dec.1672).
Wa.

Kaine, Benjamin, of Glasgow, Scotland. (Father of Boston, New
England). Administration with will to next of kin Simon
Bradstreet. (May 1662). Wa.

Kebby, John, of St. Benet Fink, London. (Brother Henry Kebby
in New England). Probate to relict Joan Kebby. (May 1642).
Wa.

Keich, Simon, of Virginia. Administration to relict Sarah
Keich. (Aug. 1655).

Keech, Simon, of Stepney, Middlesex, who died in Virginia,
bachelor. Administration with will to Ellis Kelly of St.
Michael Cornhill, London, merchant, attorney for sisters
Mary and Joanna Keech, Elizabeth Woodnett, widow, and Sarah
Tilly, widow. (Aug. 1688).

Kellond, John, of Paingsford, Devon. (Son Thomas Kellond of
Boston, New England). Probate to son John Kellond. (July
1679). Wa.

Kelway, Walter, of Chelmsford, Essex. (Daughters Margaret
Mountague, Melcas Snow and Mary Lane in New England).
Probate to relict Joan Kelway. (Feb. 1651). Sh.Wa.

Kemb, Margaret, of St. Saviour, Southwark, Surrey, widow.
(Son Thomas Kembe in Virginia). Probate to Sarah Feake.
(Nov. 1665). Wa.

Kempe, Richard, of Kich Neck, Virginia. Probate to relict
Elizabeth Lunsford alias Kempe; other executors daughter
Elizabeth Kempe and Ralfe Wormley having died. (Dec. 1656).
Sh.

Kempster, John, of Plaistow, Essex. (Cousin John Wilkins of
Boston, New England). Probate to James Whitton with similar
powers reserved to Edward Withers, Philip Perry and Thomas
Aunger. (June 1687). Wa.

Kennedy, Adam, of Antigua, (intending for New York). Probate
to William Gordon. (Aug. 1698).

Kent, Elizabeth, of Sunning, Berkshire, widow. (Brother Carey
Latham in New England). Probate to Catherine Hunt. (June
1680). Wa.

Kestin, Francis, of St. Olave, Southwark, Surrey. (Brother
Thomas Kestin in Virginia). Probate to relict Elizabeth
Kestin. (Jan. 1667). Wi.

Key, Isaac, of St. Saviour, Southwark, Surrey, who died in
Virginia. Administration to *(not stated)*. (May 1680).

Kidby, John, who died on ship *Providence* coming from Virginia.
Administration to relict Joane Kidby. (July 1655).

Kineman, John - see Clarke.

King, Edward, of Virginia, bachelor. Administration to sister
Mariane Carlton, widow. (July 1688).

King, Peter, of Shaston, Dorset. (Brother Thomas King in New
England). Probate to son Peter King. (Dec. 1658). Wa.

Kingswell, Edward, of St. Sepulchre, Newgate, London. (Goods
in Virginia). Probate to brother and sister Roger Wingate
and Dorothy his wife. (Apr. 1636). Wi.

Kinsey, Ralph, of St. Botolph Aldersgate, London. (Lands in
Pennsylvania). Probate to William Kinsey and Robert Browne.
(June 1682).
Knight, George, of Virginia, bachelor. Administration to
sister Frances, wife of Charles Bayley. (May 1684).
Knight, Henry, of Maryland. Probate to Robert Day. (Jan.1675).
Knight, Mary, of Virginia, spinster. Administration to mother
Elizabeth Knight. (June 1685). Revoked on her death and
granted to sister Catherine, wife of Richard Shaw. (June
1686).
Knight, Nathaniel, of James Town, Virginia. Administration to
brother Joseph Knight; father Samuel Knight renouncing.
(Sept. 1678).
Knight, Toby, of New England, bachelor. Administration to
Nicholas Phelps, guardian of nephew and nieces Elizabeth,
Margaret and John Ellys, and to Alice and John Phelps.
(Sept. 1660).

Laight, Edward, of Virginia, bachelor. Administration to
mother Elizabeth Laight. (Aug. 1679).
Lancaster, Elisha, of Bristol who died at Virginia. Admini-
stration to relict Elianor Lancaster. (Nov. 1694).
Lancaster, Robert, of Bristol, surgeon, who died at sea.
(Goods in Virginia). Probate to mother Anne Lancaster,
widow. (Aug. 1685). Wa.Wi.
Lane, Margaret, of London, widow. (Sister Martha, wife of
William Eaton in New England). Administration with will to
Elizabeth Jenkins, relict and administratrix with will of
executor Daniel Jenkins deceased. (Aug. 1667). Wa.
Lane, Thomas, of London who died in Virginia, bachelor.
Administration to brother William Lane. (July 1677).
Langhorne alias Ingoldsby, Mary, of Holborn, Middlesex, who
died at Staughton, Huntingdonshire, widow. (Nephew Oxen-
bridge in New England). Probate to Sir William Langhorne.
(Dec. 1686).
Langhorne, Thomas, of Pennsylvania. Administration to princi-
pal creditor Seth Flower. (Dec. 1689).
Langley, John, MD, of St. Saviour, Southwark, Surrey. (Daughter
Margaret Day in Maryland). Probate to relict Thomazine
Langley. (Feb. 1699).
Langston, William, of Virginia. Administration to brother Henry
Langston during minority and absence of children Anthony,
Judith, Francis and Mary Langston. (Dec. 1659).
Larabee, John, of New England. Probate to Elizabeth Crawford.
(June 1694). Wa.
Larkins, James, of New York. Administration to Lancaster Symms,
now husband and attorney of relict Catherine Symms alias
Larkins. (Feb. 1697).
Larrence, Charles, of Boston, New England. Administration to
principal creditor John Baker. (Feb. 1687).
Lathbury, John, of London who died at Virginia. Probate to
John Drewry. (July 1655). Sh.Wi.
Laurence, James, of Kingston, Warwickshire, who died at Virginia,
bachelor. Administration to mother Mary, wife of William
Russell. (Dec. 1694).

Lawne, Christopher, of Blandford, Dorset, (now in Virginia).
Administration with will to William Willis during minority
of sons Lovewell and Symon Lawne. (June 1620). Sh.
Lawrie, Gawen, Governor of East Jersey. Administration with
will to grandson by a daughter Obediah Haige; executrix
Johanna Watt renouncing. (Sept. 1697).
Leigh, Humphrey, who died overseas (bound for Virginia), bachelor.
Administration with will to sister Judith Skinn alias Leigh;
no executor having been named. (Mar. 1663).
Lee, John, of Charles Town, New England, who died at sea on
ship *Swallow*. Administration with nuncupative will to Giles
Tifield; no executor having been named. (June 1692). Wa.
Ley, Lawrence, of St. Martin, Ironmonger Lane, London. (Lands
in Virginia). Probate to relict Emma Ley. (Apr. 1625).Wa.
Lee, Richard, of Stratford Langton, Essex, who died at Virginia.
Probate to Thomas Griffith and John Lockey with similar
powers reserved to John and Richard Lee. (Jan. 1665).
Lee, Richard, of St. Michael Bassishaw, London. (Goods in
Virginia). Probate to Samuel Stone and Richard Cock. (Jan.
1667). Wa. See NGSQ 62/45, 63/42.
Leigh - see Lee.
Le Reux, Peeter, of St. Benet Sheerhog, London, who died at
Virginia. Administration to uncle Phillipp Le Reux. (Jan.
1654).
Letchworth, Thomas the younger, citizen and fishmonger of London
who died in Virginia. Probate to father Thomas Letchworth.
(Mar. 1657).
Ley - see Lee.
Lidget, Charles, formerly of Boston, New England, who died at
St. Bride, London. Special administration with will to
John Hester with similar powers reserved to relict Mary Lidget.
(May 1698). Further grant May 1701. Wa.
Lisle, Dame Alicia, of Moyles Court, Hampshire. (Daughter
Bridget in New England). Probate to Tarphena Lloyd with
similar powers reserved to other executors. (Nov. 1689). Wa.
Little, Basill, of London who died in Virginia, bachelor.
Administration to only sister Anne Little; mother Mary Little
renouncing. (July 1658).
Littleboy, Laurence, of Virginia. Administration by order pen-
ding suit between John Allen and Michael Bayley to said John
Allen of Virginia. (June 1653). See NGSQ 61/261.
Lluellin, Daniel, of Chelmsford, Essex. (Lands in Virginia).
Probate to Thomas Vervell, James Jauncy, Giles Sussex and
William Walker. (Mar. 1664). Wi.
Lloyd, Alexander, of Bristol who died in Virginia. Administra-
tion to brother and next of kin Lewis Lloyd. (Jan. 1679).
Lloyd, Edward, of Whitechapel, Middlesex, but formerly of Mary-
land. Probate to relict Grace Lloyd. (July 1696).
Lloyd, Elizabeth, of Elizabeth River, Lower Norfolk, Virginia,
widow. Probate to brother-in-law Thomas Eavans. (June 1657).
Sh.Wi.
Lloyd alias Carter, Elizabeth, of Richmond Co., Virginia.
Administration to husband John Lloyd. (Oct. 1694).
Lloyd, Henrietta Maria, of Talbot Co., Maryland, widow. Admini-
stration to son Richard Benett pending receipt of a copy of
will. (Sept. 1697).
Lloyd, James, of Boston, New England. Probate to Francis Brinley
and John Nelson. (Apr. 1696). Wa.
Lloyde, John, of Virginia. Administration to daughter Mary
Lloyde. "Poor." (Aug. 1653).
Lloyd, Simon, of Virginia. Probate to Robert Conway. (July
1657).

Lloyd, William, of Redcliffe, Bristol. (Lands in Rhode Island).
Probate to relict Alice Lloyd. (Feb. 1676). Wa.

Lloyd, William, of Westminster, Middlesex, who died at Virginia,
bachelor. Administration to principal creditor William
Binsley. (May 1678).

Lluwellin - see Llewellin.

Locky, Edward, of Virginia, planter, who died at St. Catherine
Creechurch, London. Limited administration to Richard
Walton, scissor merchant, with inventory of goods in London.
(Oct. 1667).

Longman, Richard, of Virginia, bachelor. Administration to
brother James Longman. (May 1679).

Low, Richard, of Virginia, bachelor. Administration to mother
Jane Allen alias Low. (Sept. 1655).

Lucas, Bridget, of St. Stephen, Coleman Street, London.
(Kinswoman Mary Bishopp in Virginia). Probate to son Ralph
Leeke. (Nov. 1657). Sh.Wa.

Lucas, Peter, of Chipping Norton, Oxfordshire, who died at
Virginia, bachelor. Administration to brother David Lucas;
mother Sarah Lucas alias Bolgye renouncing. (Mar. 1693).

Lucas, Robert, of Hitchin, Hertfordshire. (Lands in New England).
Probate to George Draper and Simon Lucas. (Feb. 1679). Wa.

Lucas, Thomas the younger, of Virginia, bachelor. Administration
to cousin and next of kin John Lucas. (July 1675).

Ludham, Edmund, of Ratcliff, Middlesex, who died at Virginia.
Administration to relict Margaret Ludham. (July 1655).

Ludlow, Francis, of Horningham, Wiltshire, who died in Virginia.
Administration to William Richards, uncle and guardian of
children Francis and William Ludlow until they are 21.
(July 1671).

Ludlow, George, of York, Virginia. Administration with will by
order to Roger Ludlow, father of nephews and nieces Jonathan,
Joseph, Roger, Anne, Mary and Sarah Ludlow during their
minority; no executor having been named. (Aug. 1656)
Sh.Wa.Wi.

Ludlowe, George, of Hedingham Sible, Essex, who died at Virginia,
bachelor. Administration to mother Mary, wife of Peter Temple.
(Oct. 1683).

Ludlow, John, of Virginia, bachelor. Administration to brother
Francis Ludlow. (Sept. 1664).

Ludwell, Thomas, of Bruton, Somerset, who died in Virginia.
Probate to John Jeffries, Edward Leman and John Browne.
(Jan. 1679). Wa.

Luscombe, Thomas, of Boston, New England. Administration to
Edward Hull, attorney for principal creditor Benjamin Mountford at Boston. (Sept. 1699).

Lymbrie, George, of St. Katherine by Tower, London, (who died
in Virginia). Administration to principal creditor William
Day. (Sept. 1637). See NGSQ 67/63.

Lyndon, Augustine, (shipwright of Boston, New England), who
died at Shadwell, Middlesex. Probate to John Johnson.
(Aug. 1699). Wa.

Lyon, John, formerly of New England but late of ship *Elizabeth*
in State service. Administration with will to Alice Linsey.
(Oct. 1658).

Macaire, Francis, who died overseas, (will dated Charles Town, Carolina). Probate to Cephas Tutet. (Apr. 1691).

MeCrow, John, of Shadwell, Stepney, Middlesex, who died at Virginia. Administration to relice Luce Johnson alias Jonson alias MeaCrow. (Mar. 1658).

Major, Jerman, of St. Faith Virgin, London. (Cousin Ann Jones in New England). Probate to relict Deborah Major and son Thomas Major. (Oct. 1661). Wa.

Mallett alias Wolseley, Winifred, of Maryland, widow. Administration with will to principal creditor James Annis; niece and executrix Mary Bilookes having died and surviving legatee Helen Spratt, wife of Bishop of Rochester, renouncing. (Mar. 1697).

Mallory, Phillip, of Virginia who died at Whitechapel, Middlesex. Probate to John Whitty with similar powers reserved to nephew Roger Mallory. (July 1661). Sm.Wi.

Manfield, George, (of Virginia) who died overseas, bachelor. Probate to John Beale. (July 1670). Wi.

Manstidge, Robert, of Taunton, Somerset, who died overseas. (Goods in Virginia). Probate to brothers and sister Jone, William, Isaack and Emanuel Manstidge. (Feb. 1630).

Maplet, John, of Bath, Somerset. (Sister Mary Gorton in New England). Probate to relict Anne Maplet. (Feb. 1671). Wa.

Maplet alias Mayplett, Mary, of St. Giles Cripplegate, London, widow. (Daughter Mary, wife of Samuel Gorton in New England). Probate to son John Maplet. (Apr. 1647). Wa.

Maplisden, Joan, of Westminster, Middlesex. (Kisman John Lee of Virginia). Probate to husband Peter Maplisden. (Dec. 1656). Wa.

Mapson, Thomas, of Bethnal Green, Middlesex. (Granddaughter Susanna Mapson feared lost on voyage to New England). Probate to relict Joane Mapson with similar powers reserved to son James Mapson. (July 1660).

Marsh, William, of Charles Town, New England, who died at Stepney, Middlesex, from H.M.S. *Mary*. Probate to Robert Robinson; grant of August 1695 to creditor John Casey now revoked. (Sept. 1695).

Marshall, Samuel, of Great Waltham, Essex, who died in New England. Administration to son John Marshall. (Feb. 1694).

Martin, Henry, of Wapping, Middlesex, mariner. (Lands in New England). Probate to relict Margaret Martin. (Feb. 1662). Wa.

Martin, John, (of New England), who died at sea on ship *Jersey*, bachelor. Administration with will to James Babson; no executor having been named. (Feb. 1674). Wa.

Martin, John, of Stepney, Middlesex. (Lands in Virginia). Probate to Micajah Perry. (Oct. 1684). Wi.

Martin, Joseph, who died in King's service at sea or in Virginia, bachelor. Administration to principal creditrix Avitia Foster. (Aug. 1667).

Martyn, Nicholas, of Ratcliffe, Middlesex, who died coming from Virginia. Administration with nuncupative will to Mary Farthing; no executor having been named. (*Listed in Administration Act Book*). (Nov. 1656). Sh.

Martin, Richard, of Chatham, Kent. (Son Richard Martin in New England). Probate to relict Rose Martin. (June 1659) Wa.

Mascal, Giles, of Wartling, Sussex, clerk. (Son Edward to go to New England, Virginia or Barbados). Probate to son Samuel Mascal. (July 1652). Sh.

Mason, John, of Westminster, Middlesex. (Goods in New England). Probate to relict Anne Mason. (Dec. 1635). Sh.

Mason, Thomas, of Virginia, bachelor. Administration to sister
Anne, wife of Peter Booker. (Jan. 1675).
Mather, Gilbert, of Whitechapel, Middlesex, who died in Virginia.
Administration to relict Mary Mather. (July 1668).
Mather, Thomas, (bound for New York), who died at sea, bachelor.
Probate to sister Martha Coppocke. (Mar. 1687).
Mathew, Thomas, of Holborn, Middlesex. (Daughter Mary in Mary-
land). Probate to relict Mary Mathew. (Mar. 1667). Wi.
Matthewes, Elizabeth, of St. Mary Woolnoth, London, who died in
New England. Probate to Susan Lansdale with similar powers
reserved to John Lansdale. (Nov. 1690).
Mavell, Richard, of Hanly Castle, Worcestershire, who died at
Virginia, bachelor. Administration to brother and next of
kin Thomas Mavell. (Aug. 1678).
Mawer, George, of Durham Bishopric who died in Virginia.
Administration to daughter Rahael Mawer; relict Hellen Mawer
renouncing. (Sept. 1682).
Maye, Joseph, of St. Mary Strand, Middlesex. (Cousin Cornelius
Maye in Virginia). Probate to brother Phineas Maye. (Feb.
1636). Wa.Wi.
Maynard, John, of King Street, Wapping, Middlesex, who died at
Virginia. Administration to relict Mary Maynard. (Mar.1660).
Mayow, John, doctor of laws of Bath, Somerset, who died at St.
Paul, Covent Garden, Middlesex. (Daughter Mary Slater of New
York). Administration with will to relict Alice Mayow;
executor Thomas Mayow having died. (June 1680). See NGSQ
64/48.
Mayplett - see Maplet.
Mead, John, of Wapping, Whitechapel, Middlesex. (Goods in Mary-
land). Limited administration to Peter Renou, owner of ship
Samuel and Henry formerly named Europe. (Oct. 1694).
Meeres, Stephen, of Boston, New England, who died on H.M.S.
Warspight, bachelor. Administration to principal creditor
John Cockburne. (Oct. 1689).
Meese, Henry, of St. Catherine Creechurch, London. (Lands in
Virginia). Probate to relict Anne Meese. (Apr. 1682).
Menefie, George, of Buckland, Virginia. Probate to relict Mary
Menefie. (Feb. 1647). Sh.Sm.Wi.
Mercer, William, citizen and haberdasher of London. (Brother
Burrandine Mercer in Virginia). Probate to brother Walter
Mercer. (Mar. 1654). Wi.
Meriman, George, citizen and cooper of London. (Son in New
England). Probate to son John Meriman. (May 1656). Sh.Wa.
Meriton, Joshua, of Virginia. Administration to relict Mary
Meriton. (Oct. 1674).
Merriken, Hugh, of Maryland. Administration to relict Anne
Merriken. (Feb. 1698).
Merritt, Richard, of Stepney, Middlesex, who died in Virginia.
Administration to principal creditor Benjamin Andrews. (Jan.
1692).
Mew, Samuel, of St. Mildred Poultry, London. (Brother Ellis Mew
and sister Sarah Cowper of New England). Probate to Edward
Bilton and Thomas Lambe. (May 1671).
Michell alias Townsend, Joane, of Virginia. Administration to
Isaac Plavier, father and guardian of nephew and nieces James,
Judith and Anne Plavier. (Sept. 1661).
Middleton, Philip, of St. Olave, Southwark, Surrey. (Daughter
Hannah, wife of Edward Pomfast in New England). Probate to
daughter Mary, wife of George Seale. (Dec. 1650). Wa.
Middleton, Robert, of Virginia, bachelor. Administration with
will to Thomas Babb during absence of brother William Middle-
ton; no executor having been named. (July 1627). Sh.Wa.Wi.

Middleton, Thomas, of London. (Lands in New England). Probate
   to son Benjamin Middleton. (Dec. 1672)
Mills, Thomas, of Exeter, Devon. (Son William in Virginia).
   Probate to relict Honor Mills. (Sept. 1653).
Mynterne, John, of Manigo, Virginia. Administration with will
   to relict Alice Mynterne; no executor having been named.
   (Jan. 1619). Wi.
Monylockes, James, of Ratcliffe, Stepney, Middlesex, who died
   at Virginia. Administration to relict Alice Monylockes.
   (Apr. 1668).
Moody, John, of island of Virginia. Administration to Susan
   Poynts, ?sister of relict Rebecca Moody during her absence.
   (Sept. 1681).
Moone, George, of Fremington, Devon, mariner, (who died at
   Virginia). Probate by sentence to relict Alice Moone.
   (Nov. 1680).
Moone, Patrick, of Shadwell, Middlesex, who died at Virginia.
   Administration to relict Joanna Moone. (Dec. 1679).
Morcombe, Johnson, of Bideford, Devon, who died in Virginia.
   Administration to relict Dorcas Morcombe. (May 1680).
Mordant, George, of Felmingham, Norfolk, (adventurer to Vir-
   ginia). Probate to nephew Henry Mordant and Talbot Pepys
   with similar powers reserved to Ralph Ward and Thomas Utbert.
   (Nov. 1633). Sh.Wi.
Mordoch - see Murdoch.
More, Mary, of Kennington, Surrey. (Son Samuel Hardy in New
   England). Probate to Edward Palmer and Isaac Gildersleeve.
   (Oct. 1678). Wa.
Morecroft, Edmund, (of Virginia) who died overseas. Probate
   to sister Elizabeth Morecroft with similar powers reserved
   to sister Mary Morecroft. (June 1639). Sh.Sm.Wi.
Morgan, George, who died at sea or in Virginia, bachelor.
   Probate to Richard Knewstubb. (Apr. 1669).
Morgan, Richard, of Islington, Middlesex. Administration to
   George Smith, attorney for only child Jude Morgan in Virginia.
   (June 1661).
Morris, Judith, of Dedham, Essex, widow. (Kinsman Stephen Hart
   in New England). Probate to John Morris with similar powers
   reserved to Clement Fenne. (Mar. 1646). Wa.
Morris, Thomas, of Shadwell, Middlesex, who died at Virginia
   on ship *Dunbarton*. Administration to principal creditor
   Humphrey Cock; relict Margaret Morris renouncing. (June
   1687).
Morton, John, who died at Carolina. Probate to Robert Cuthbert
   the younger. (May 1699) Further grant March 1706.
Morton, Richard, of Virginia, bachelor. Administration to
   principal creditrix Alice Usher. (May 1663).
Morton, Thomas, of Cliffords Inn, London. (Lands in New
   England), died overseas. Probate to niece Sarah Wilson
   alias Bruce. (Aug. 1660). Sh.
Moulson, Peter, of St. Bartholomew the Less, London. (Brother
   Foulke Moulson in Virginia). Probate to Margaret Blague.
   (June 1674).
Moult, William, of London who died at Accawacke, Virginia.
   Administration with will to brother Francis Moult; no
   executor having been named. (June 1657).
Moulton, Foulk, of Westover, Virginia. Administration to niece
   by a brother Mary, wife of Daniel Kerye. (Nov. 1679).
Mountgomery, James, of James River, Virginia, who died at St.
   Catherine, Creechurch, London. Probate to William Wilson
   with similar powers reserved to Robert Wilson. (Dec. 1697).
   Wa.

Muire, James, of Virginia. Administration to principal creditor
    William Jefferys. (July 1689).
Mullins, William, of Virginia, (of Plymouth, New England), who
    died overseas. Administration with will to daughter Sarah
    Blunden alias Mullins of Dorking, Surrey; no executor
    having been named. (July 1621). Wa.
Mundell, John, of Newcastle, Pennsylvania, who died at Boston,
    merchant. Probate to brother and surviving executor William
    Mundell. (Apr. 1697).
Munford, William, of Virginia who died in London, bachelor.
    Administration to brother John Munford. (Sept. 1678).
Mordoch, David, of New York. Administration to sister Jane
    Mordoch during absence of relict Mary Mordoch. (Nov. 1687).
Musgrave, Michael, of Virginia who died at St. Sepulchre, London.
    Probate to Thomas Musgrave with similar powers reserved to
    William Newton. (Jan. 1698). Wi.
Mynterne - see Minterne.

Nall, William, of Boston, New England, who died on ship *Green-
    wich*, bachelor. Probate to Henry Causton. (Jan. 1696).
Neale alias Oneale, John, of Stepney, Middlesex, who died at
    Virginia. Administration to principal creditor Richard
    Rawlins; relict Elizabeth Neale renouncing. (Sept. 1682).
Neale, Thomas, of Meryland. Administration to brother John
    Neale. (Aug. 1675).
Nedham, James, of island of Virginia, bachelor. Administration
    to mother Barabara Nedham. (Feb. 1677). Revoked on her
    death and granted to brother and next of kin George Nedham.
    (Jan. 1678).
Neeve, Mary, of Virginia, spinster. Probate to sister Sarah
    Lewis. (Jan. 1674).
Nelson, Robert, of Carolina, bachelor. Probate to Dorcas Wellin
    with similar powers reserved to Thomas Wellin. (Jan. 1683).
Nelson, Thomas, of Rowhay, Essex Co., New England. Probate to
    wife's uncle Richard Dummer with similar powers reserved to
    Richard Bellingham. (Feb. 1651). Sh.Wa.
Nevett, Hugh, of Virginia, bachelor. Administration with will
    to nephew and next of kin John Nevett; executors George
    Seaton and John Throckmorton being dead. (Oct. 1680).
Nevett, Samuel, of London who died at Virginia, bachelor.
    Administration to brother and sister John and Alice Nevett.
    (Aug. 1680).
Nevill, John, Vice-Admiral, of St. Margaret, Westminster,
    Middlesex, who died at Virginia. Probate to relict Mary
    Nevill. (Nov. 1697).
Newdigate alias Newgate, Nathaniel, of Greenwich, Kent. (Brother-
    in-law Edward Jackson of New England). Probate to relict
    Isabel Newdigate.. (Sept. 1668). New grant November 1673.
    Wa.
Newell, Jonathan, of Virginia. Administration to principal
    creditor John Randall. (Mar. 1675).
Newgate, Nathaniel - see Newdigate.
Newman, Samuel, of Boston, New England, who died in Barbados.
    Administration to creditors John Newman and Thomas Dodge.
    (Dec. 1696).

Newton, Francis, of London, grocer, (bound for New England).
Probate to Anthony Stanford with similar powers reserved
to John Berry and Joseph Wilson. (Jan. 1662). Wa.Wi.

Newton, John, of Colyton, Devon. (Children Anthony and Joane
in New England). Probate to daughter Mary, wife of Thomas
Stocker. (Apr. 1647). Wa.

Newton, Joseph, of ship *Dreadnought*, (bound to Virginia).
Probate to Richard Martin. (Oct. 1694).

Nicholls, Richard, of St. Olave, Southwark, Surrey, who died
on ship *Susanna* in Virginia. Administration to relict
Tabitha Nicholls. (May 1692).

Nicholson, George, of Boston, New England, who died in Virginia.
Administration to brother Edward Nicholson during absence
in New England of relict Hannah Nicholson. (July 1692).

Nicholson, John, (of Maryland) who died on ship *Anne*. Probate
to relict Catherine Nicholson. (Aug. 1693).

Nicholson, Robert,, of London, merchant, who died overseas,
(to be buried in Barbados or Virginia). Administration
with will to father Francis Nicholson; John Corbin and
John Young renouncing. (Aug. 1652). Sh.Wa.

Nicholson, Thomas, of Marblehead, New England. Administration
to Thomas Newton, attorney for relict Elizabeth, now wife
of Richard Crafts, during her absence. (Jan. 1697).

Noore, John, of Stepney, Middlesex, (bound for Virginia).
Probate to relict Anne Noore. (July 1693).

Norcross, Jeremiah, of Walsingham, Norfolk. (Goods in New
England). Probate to son Nathaniel Norcross. (Apr. 1658).
Sh.Sm.

Norcrosse, Rev. Nathaniel, of St. Dunstan in East, London.
(Goods in New England). Probate to relict Mary Norcrosse;
Thomas Brookes and Edward Henninge renouncing. (Oct. 1662).
Wa.

Norrington, William, master of frigate *?Leart* who died at
Virginia. Administration to relict Rebecca Norrington.
(July 1697).

Northcote, Catherine, of Hoxton, Middlesex, widow. (Kinswoman
Jane Poole and her son Theophilus Poole of Boston, New
England). Probate to Thomas Rowe with similar powers
reserved to John and William Rowe. (Aug. 1685). Wa.

Norton, Tobias, of Virginia. Administration to relict Joane
Norton. (Dec. 1658).

Norwood, Thomas, of Virginia, widower. Administration to son
Wolstenholme Norwood. "Pauper." (Nov. 1679).

Nowell, Christopher, of Leeds, Yorkshire. (Lands in New England).
Probate to Margaret Nowell. (Sept. 1657). Wa.

Nowell, Edward, of Virginia, bachelor. Administration to
Elizabeth Quint, attorney for father Edward Nowell in Cornwall.
(July 1689).

Noye, Philip, formerly of St. Buryan, late of St. Just, Cornwall.
(Adventurer in Virginia). Probate to mother Sarah Noye.
(June 1650). Wi.

Noyes, Anne, of Cholderton, Wiltshire, widow. (Sons James and
Nicholas Noyes in New England). Probate to Robert Rede.
(Apr. 1658). Sh.Wa.

Noyes, Peter, of Sudbury, New England. Probate to William and
John Crouch, attornies for sisters Mary Mountjoy, Dorothy,
wife of Samuel Parris, Sarah, wife of Thomas Frinck, and
Ester Noyes, all in New England. (Sept. 1699).

Oker, Abraham, of ship *Lord Salsberry* who died at sea on ship *Bendish* (bound for Virginia), bachelor. Administration to principal creditrix Elianor Hitchcock; executor James Farthing renouncing. (Aug. 1667).

Oliver, Joseph, of Virginia, bachelor. Administration to principal creditor James Emerson. (Sept. 1688).

Oneale, John - see Neale.

Osborne, Samuel, of St. Olave, Southwark, Surrey, who died at Carolina. Administration to principal creditor Chaning Radcliffe; relict Sarah Osborne renouncing. (Apr. 1683).

Osgood, John, of Leytonstone, Essex. (Lands in New Jersey). Probate to son Salem Osgood, Theodore Ecclestone and John Hall. (June 1694). NGSQ 63/135.

Otterton, John, of Nancy Mum, Virginia. Administration to relict Mary Otterton. (June 1654).

Ottway, John, of Hersom, Surrey, who died overseas, (bound for New England), bachelor. Administration with will to Elizabeth, wife of Thomas Ernall. (Mar. 1670).

Owen, William, of Limehouse, Middlesex, who died at Virginia. Administration to Anne Bascombe, guardian of only child William Owen during his minority. (Oct. 1655).

Owen, William, of Carolina. Administration to brother Henry Owen. (Dec. 1690).

Oxenbridge, William, of St. Alban, Wood Street, London. (Bequest to help Indians in New England). Probate to son Clement Oxenbridge; son John Oxenbridge renouncing. (Nov. 1651). Wa.

Palmer, Edward, of Leamington, Gloucestershire, who died in London. (Lands in Virginia and New England). Probate to son Giles Palmer. (Dec. 1624). Wa.

Palmer, Giles, of Bridgenorth, Shropshire. (Lands in Virginia). Probate to Edward Palmer. (June 1637). Wi.

Pargiter, John, of St. Martin in Fields, Middlesex. (Cousin Sarah Lovell in Virginia). Probate to sons John and Samuel Pargiter. (Feb. 1688). Wa.

Parke, Daniel, of London who died in Virginia. Special administration with will to son Daniel Parke with similar powers reserved to James Bray and Robert Cobb; executor Edward Carter renouncing. (Sept. 1679). Wi.

Parke, William, who died overseas. (Bequest to Adam Thorowgood of Virginia). Administration with will to relict Sarah Parke during minority of son William Parke. (Aug. 1634). Sh.Wi.

Parker, Alexander, of St. Edmund, Lombard Street, London. (Lands in Pennsylvania). Probate to Mary Parker and Prudence Wager. (Apr. 1689).

Parker, Dorothy, of Mildenhall, Wiltshire. (Son Thomas Parker in New England). Probate to Benjamin Woodbridge with similar powers reserved to daughter Sarah Bayly. (Apr. 1650). Sh.Wa.

Parker, Joseph, of St. Pancras, Soper Lane, London. (Brother James Parker in New England). Probate to relict Anne Parker with similar powers reserved to daughter Elizabeth Parker. (Dec. 1644). Wa.

Parker, Judith, of New England, widow. Probate to Robert
Manning of Ipswich, Suffolk. (May 1649). Sh.Wa.
Parker, Robert, of Bosham, Sussex. (Lands in Virginia).
Probate to son George Parker. (Apr. 1673). Wi.
Parker, William, of Stepney, Middlesex. (Goods in Maryland).
Probate to relict Grace Parker. (July 1673).
Parkes, Andrew, of London, haberdasher, who died overseas.
(Brother John Parkes in Virginia). Probate to aunt Ellen
Warden of Christ's Hospital, London, widow. (Feb. 1630).
Parkhurst, George, of Ipswich, Suffolk, (bound to Virginia).
Administration with will to relict Elizabeth Parkhurst;
no executor having been named. (Oct. 1635).
Parks, Edward, of St. Matthew, Friday Street, London. (Lands
in New England). Probate to Thomas Plampin and John Bagnall.
(Jan. 1651). Revoked on their death and administration
granted to son John Parks. (Mar. 1673). Revoked on his
death and granted to relict Mary Cawley alias Parks. (Nov.
1681). Sh.
Parry, John, (of Virginia) who died overseas, bachelor.
Administration with nuncupative will to brother William
Parry; no executor having been named. (July 1638).
Sh.Sm.Wi.
Parsons, Robert, of frigate *James* who died in Virginia, bache-
lor. Administration by order to mother Sarah Butler alias
Parsons. (June 1655).
Parsons, William, of Newcastle upon Tyne, bachelor. Administra-
tion to Samuel Sheafe, attorney for brother Humphrey and
Joseph Parsons at Boston, New England. (Mar. 1696).
Partridge, Samuel, of Rapah Hannocke, Virginia. Administration
to sister Sarah Partridge alias Wilson. (July 1676).
Further grant January 1690.
Pate (*Peate* in calendar), John, of Virginia, bachelor. Admini-
stration to brother Edward Pate. (Mar. 1673).
Pate, Richard, of Virginia. Administration to nephew John
Pate. (Oct. 1657).
Paul, Stephen, of New England who died on ship *New Castle
Merchant*. Administration to principal creditor Samuel
Hockaday. (May 1696).
Payne, Mathew, of Pennsylvania, widower. Administration to
son Edmund Payne. (Oct. 1686).
Paynter, Nicholas, of Anne Arundell Co., Maryland. Probate to
Henry Bray. (Oct. 1685).
Payton, John, of Portbury, Somerset. (Credits in Virginia and
Maryland). Probate to relict Jone Payton. (Aug. 1699). Wi.
Peake, Sir Robert, of Richmond, Surrey. (Cousin George Lyddall
in Virginia). Probate to Gregory and Benjamin Peake.
(July 1667). Wa.
Pierce, Mark, (late of New England), of London who died in
Ireland. Probate to William Viner and Robert Newman.
(June 1656). Sh.Wa.
Pearle, Richard, of Virginia, bachelor. Administration to
father and principal creditor Thomas Pearle. (Oct. 1668).
Peate, John - see Pate.
Peck, Edward, sergeant at law of Inner Temple, London. (Brother
Edward in New England). Probate to son William Peck.
(June 1676). Wa.
Pecke, Robert, of Hingham, Norfolk, clerk. (Daughter Anne,
wife of Captain John Mason of Seabrooke, New England).
Probate to Samuel Pecke. (Apr. 1658). Sh.Wa.
Peele, Elizabeth, of Maryland, spinster. Administration to
father Bartholomew Peele. (Aug. 1685).

Peer, Thomas, of St. Mary Magdalene, Bermondsey, Surrey, who
died in St. Mary's Co., Virginia, at Smith's Creek. Administration to principal creditor Ralph Norton; relict Joane
Peer renouncing. (Nov. 1670).

Pemerton, John, of Lawford, Essex. (Daughter-in-law Deborah
Goffe in New England). Probate to John Beeston. (Mar.
1654). Wa.

Pendergrass, Thomas, of Stepney, Middlesex, who died in Virginia.
Administration to relict Elizabeth Pendergrass. (Apr. 1699).

Penn, William, of Petuxant River, Maryland. Probate to relict
Elizabeth Penn. (Nov. 1697).

Pennington, James, of St. Bartholomew next Exchange, London,
who died in Maryland. Administration to principal creditor
Mathew Travers; relict Sarah Pennington renouncing. (Feb.
1679).

Pennoyer, William, of London. (Kinsman Robert Pennoyer of New
England). Probate to Richard Loton and Michael Dewison.
(Feb. 1671). Wa. See NGSQ 60/244.

Percey - see Persey.

Percivall, Andrew, of St. Margaret, Westminster, Middlesex.
(Lands in Carolina). Probate to relict Essex Percivall.
(Mar. 1696). Further grant June 1730).

Perdrian, Lewis, of Carolina who died at Barbados. Probate to
sister Judith, wife of Paul Faneuil; no executor having
been named. (July 1697).

Perdrian, Peter, of Carolina, bachelor. Administration to
brother Daniel Perdrian. (Apr. 1693).

Perry, John, of St. Antholin, London, who died overseas, (at
James City, Virginia). Probate to brother Richard Perry.
(Apr. 1629). Sh.

Perry, Robert, of Bristol, clerk. (Nephew Robert Perry in
Virginia). Probate to relict Elizabeth Perry. (July 1652).
Sh.Wa.Wi.

Perry, Thomas, of Virginia. Administration to sister Margaret,
wife of Bartholomew Terrett. (July 1670).

Persey, Abraham, of Persey's Hundred, Virginia. Administration
with will to daughter Mary Hill; relict Frances Persey
having died. (May 1633). Sh.Wi.

Percey, Richard, of ship *Two Brothers* (sick in Virginia).
Probate to relict Annis Percey. (Mar. 1654). Sh.

Petty, Francis, of ship *Hope* (bound for New England). Probate
to relict Sarah Petty. (Sept. 1693).

Phelps, Edward, of Virginia, bachelor. Administration to sister
Mary, wife of Jonathan Davis. (May 1678).

Philipps, Caleb, of New England who died on H.M.S. *Expedition*.
Administration with will to James Harris of Bermondsey,
Surrey, attorney for relict Elizabeth Philipps. (Jan. 1693).

Phillips, Lewis, of Huntingdon. (Cousin John Throckmorton in
Virginia). Probate to William Hally. (Mar. 1670).

Phippen, George - see Fitzpen.

Phipping, William, of Wedmore, Somerset. (Daughter Judah in New
England). Probate to daughter Elizabeth, wife of John Addams.
(Nov. 1650). Sh.

Phipps, John, of London. (Son Henry Phipps in Maryland).
Probate to son Henry Phipps. (Oct. 1673). Sh.

Phipps, Sir William, Governor of New England who died in London.
Probate to relict Lady Mary Phipps. (Jan. 1697). Sm.Wa.

Pierce - see Pearce.

Pilkington, William, of Virginia. Administration to brother
Sir Arthur Pilkington. (Oct. 1641).

Pindar, William, Rector of Mottisfount, Hampshire, clerk.
(Kinsman Thomas Shingleton alias Lea in Virginia). Administration with will by decree to Sarah Pindar, mother of

grandson Samuel Pindar during his minority; no executor having been named. (Feb. 1627). Wa.

Pinder, Mathew, of Virginia, bachelor. Administration to brother William Pinder. (June 1675).

Plowden, Sir Edmund, of Wanstead, Hampshire, Captain-General of New Albion, America. Probate to Henry Sharpe. (July 1659). Sh.

Plowden, Thomas, of Lasham, Hampshire. (Lands in Virginia). Probate to relict Thomasine Plowden. (Sept. 1698).

Pond, Samuel, of Virginia. Limited administration to Micajah Perry of St. Catherine Creechurch, London, merchant, attorney for relict Rebecca, now wife of Thomas Mountfort. (July 1698).

Pope, Thomas, of St. Philip & James, Bristol, merchant. (Lands in Virginia). Probate to Richard Gotley with similar powers reserved to Charles Jones. (Oct. 1685).

Poppleton, William, of St. Giles Cripplegate, London. (Lands in Virginia). Probate to William Emerson with similar powers reserved to William Thorowgood and Richard Buffington. (July 1632). Wi.

Pordage, Joshua, of St. Botolph Bishopsgate, London. (Son George Pordage of Boston, New England). Probate to Thomas Major. (June 1691). Wa.

Portman, Robert, who died overseas. (Goods in Virginia). Probate to sister Margaret Portman. (Aug. 1654). Sh.

Potts, Theophilus, of Virginia, bachelor. Administration to sister Sarah, wife of Edward Huit. (July 1678).

Pouls alias Poulson, Paul, of Virginia, bachelor. Administration to principal creditor Andrew Anderson. (May 1684).

Poulter, Hannah - see Wallin.

Pountes, John, citizen and clothworker of London. (Interests in Virginia fisheries and intending for Virginia). Probate to Sir Thomas Merry. (June 1624). Wa.

Powell, John, of St. Michael, Crooked Lane, London. (Cousin in Virginia). Probate to relict Ann Powell. (Dec. 1624). Wi.

Powell, John, of New England who died on frigate *Moncke* at sea, bachelor. Administration to principal creditor Thomas Raye. (Feb. 1673).

Powell, Richard, of Virginia. Administration to uncle and next of kin William Powell. (Nov. 1654).

Powell, William the elder, of Virginia. Administration to brother William Powell. (Aug. 1651).

Power, Thomas, of St. Margaret Lothbury, London, who died at Virginia. Administration to son Benjamin Power. (July 1686).

Powys, Thomas, of London who died at Boston, New England, bachelor. Administration to brother Richard Powys. (Sept. 1684).

Predix, Gabriel, of Virginia. Administration with will to principal creditor Peter Senth; relict Susanna Predix renouncing. (July 1697).

Preston, Richard, of Potuxent, Maryland. Administration with will to son James Preston during absence overseas of executors Peter Sharpe, Thomas Taylor, William Berry and John Meares. (Aug. 1670).

Prewitt, Robert, of New England who died on H.M.S. *Devonshire*. Administration to son Robert Prewitt. (May 1697).

Price, Hopkin, of Stepney, Middlesex, (late of Virginia). Probate to Thurston Withnall. (Nov. 1679). Wi.

Price, John, of Tower Precinct, London, who died in Virginia. Administration to relict Anne Price. (May 1668).

Prise, John, of Shadwell, Middlesex, who died overseas, (bound for Virginia. Probate to relict Joanne Prise. (Sept. 1677).

Price, Richard, of St. Margaret, Westminster, Middlesex,
    citizen and vintner of London. (Adventurer in Virginia).
    Probate to relict Margaret Price. (Nov. 1630).
Price, Roger, of Virginia. Probate to son Richard Price with
    similar powers reserved to William Price. (May 1672).
Prickett, Miles, of St. Cross near Canterbury, Kent.
    (Adventurer in Virginia). Probate to brother John Prickett.
    (June 1627). Wa.
Primus, John, of H.M.S. *St. Alban's* prize, who died at Virginia,
    bachelor. Probate to Prudence Poulsen, widow. (Oct. 1697).
Prinn, Nicholas, of Stepney, Middlesex, who died at Virginia.
    Probate to relict Dorothy Prinn. (May 1684).
Prise - see Price.
Pritchard, Hesther, of Holborn, Middlesex, widow. (Granddaughter
    Elizabeth, daughter of Robert Pritchard of Virginia). Probate
    to Richard Shute with similar powers reserved to Anne Turner.
    (July 1691). Wi.
Pritts, Benedict, of ship *Merchants Delight* who died at Virginia,
    bachelor. Administration to principal creditrix Hester
    Gateley alias Getley, widow. (Sept. 1681).
Proctor, Thomas, of Stepney, Middlesex. (Goods in Virginia).
    Probate to uncle William Gray. (Nov. 1624). Revoked on
    his death and administration granted to relict Jane Proctor
    alias Squire during minority of son Samuel Proctor. (Nov.)
    Wi.
Prosser, Mathias, of St. Giles Cripplegate, London, who died in
    Virginia. Administration to grandmother Jane Prosser alias
    Pitt alias Pindar alias Sayward. (Sept. 1667).
Provoast, Elias, of New York who died at Virginia on H.M.S.
    Samuell and Henry. Administration with will to John Castle;
    no executor having been named. (June 1691).
Pryor, William, who died overseas. (Lands in Virginia).
    Probate to Jasper Clayton and Thomas Harrison during minority
    of daughters Margaret and Mary Pryor. (Apr. 1647). Revoked
    and granted to daughter Mary Pryor on her coming of age.
    (Nov. 1660). Sh.Wi.
Purkis, George, of New England who died at Algiers. Administra-
    tion to principal creditor John Lake. (Apr. 1682).
Putnam, Thomas, (bound for Virginia). Administration with will
    to Thomas Putnam during absence in Virginia of relict Dorothy
    and son Thomas Putnam. (May 1659). Wi.
Pynchon, William, of Wrasbury, Buckinghamshire. (Daughter
    Margaret Davis of Boston, sons John Pynchon and Elizar
    Holioke of New England, and goods in Virginia). Probate to
    John Wickens. (Dec. 1662). Wa.

Quicke, William, of Christ Church, London. (Lands in Virginia).
    Probate to relict Elizabeth Quicke with similar powers
    reserved to Roger Harris. (Jan. 1615). Wa.
Quiney, Richard, of St. Stephen Wallbrook, London. (Lands in
    Virginia. Probate to son Richard Quiney. (Jan. 1657).

Rainborowe, William, of St. Leonard Eastcheap, London.
(Daughter Martha, wife of Thomas Cotymore in New England).
Probate to sons Thomas and William Rainborowe. (Apr. 1642).
Wa.

Rand, James, of St. Mary Colechurch, London. (Creditor of
William Bancks in Virginia). Probate to Mary Gould, wife
of Christopher Gould; relict Grace Rand having died.
(May. 1686). Wa.

Randall, Richard, of St. Olave, Southwark, Surrey, who died at
Virginia. Administration to relict Anne Randall. (Jan. 1693).

Ratcliffe, John - see Sicklemore.

Rawlins, Edward, of New York, bachelor. Administration to
principal creditor Thomas Butler. (Feb. 1678).

Rawlins, George, of Virginia. Administration to brother Giles
Rawlins. (Jan. 1654).

Raydon, William, of Philadelphia. Probate to John Tyzack.
(Jan. 1696).

Rayment, George, of Glastonbury, Somerset. (Children William,
John and Elizabeth Rayment in New England). Probate to son
Maurice Rayment. (Oct. 1651). Sh.Sm.Wa.

Rayment, John, who died overseas (bound for Virginia). Administration with will to relict Mary Graves alias Rayment.
(Sept. 1630). Sh.Wa.

Rayner, Roger, of Burnham Abbey, Buckinghamshire. (Kinsman
John Rayner of New England). Probate to Thomas Rayner.
(Oct. 1682). Wa.

Read, George, of Whitechapel, Middlesex, who died at Virginia
on ship *Culpeper*. Probate to relict Margaret Read. (Oct.
1685).

Reed, Isaac, (of Boston, New England), who died on H.M.S.*Tyger's*
prize. Probate to Mark Poyd. (Nov. 1695).

Read, John, of Bristol who died at Virginia. Administration
with will to relict Mary Read; no executor having been named.
(July 1688). Wa.

Reade, Thomas, of Wickford, Essex. (Lands in New England).
Probate to relict Priscilla Reade. (Nov. 1662). Wa.

Reade, Thomas, who died overseas, (bound for Virginia). Probate
to brother William Reade. (June 1663). Wa.

Reed, William, of Newcastle upon Tyne. (Children George, Ralph
and Abigael in New England). Administration with will to
relict Mabell Reed. (Oct. 1656). Sh.Wa.

Read, William, (of New England) and of ship *Granado* who died at
Jamaica. Probate to Elizabeth Harlock with similar powers
reserved to John Harlock. (Sept. 1692). Wa.

Reeve(s), George, of Virginia, widower. Administration to
brother Charles Reeve(s). (Mar. 1689). Revoked on introduction of will and probate granted to same. (Apr. 1689).
Wi.

Rhodes, Nathaniel, of Virginia, bachelor. Administration by
decree to brother James Rhodes; mother Ester Rhodes, widow,
renouncing. (Sept. 1697).

Rice, Robert, of Preston, Suffolk. (Brother-in-law Samuel
Appleton of New England). Probate to Sarah Allen. Admini-
stration as of intestate of November 1638 to next of kin
William Hobart now revoked. (Feb. 1639). Wa.

Rich, Jeremiah, of Stepney, Middlesex, who died at Virginia.
Administration to relict Sarah Rich. (July 1682).

Rich, Sir Nathaniel, of Dalham, Suffolk. (Bequest to Nathaniel
Browne in New England). Probate to Edward, Viscount Mandeville. (Dec. 1636). Wa.

Richards, George, of St. Botolph Aldgate, London. (Goods in
Virginia). Probate to son Phillip Richards. (Apr. 1694).

Revoked on his death and administration granted to Sarah
Perry alias Richards, sister and administratrix of said
Phillip Richards. (Apr. 1695). Wi.

Richards, Samuel, of ship *Elizabeth* who died in Virginia on
King's service. Administration to relict Elizabeth Richards.
(Jan. 1668).

Richards, Thomas, of Alverstoke, Hampshire, who died in Virginia.
Administration to relict Mary Richards. (July 1677).

Richardson, Anthony, of Limehouse, Middlesex, who died in Virginia. Administration to relict Sarah Richardson. (Sept.
1656).

Richmond, Richard, of St. Leonard, Foster Lane, London. (Sister
Margaret Richmond in Virginia). Probate to relict Grace
Richmond. (Jan. 1685). Wa.

Ring, John, who died overseas, (bound for Virginia), bachelor.
Probate to brother Matthias Ring with similar powers reserved to Richard Atkins. (Apr. 1637). Sh.Wi.

Roane, Robert, of Chaldon, Surrey. (Son Charles Roane in
Virginia). Probate to George Perryer, Roger Lambert and
Thomas Landon. (May 1676). Wi.

Robyns, Edward, who died at Virginia. Administration to
principal creditor Francis Burroughes. (Sept. 1647).

Robins, Jeremy, of St. Martin in Fields, Middlesex. (Daughter
Rebecca Robins in Virginia). Probate to relict Sarah Robins.
(Oct. 1671). Wi.

Robinson, Maximilian, of Rotherhithe, Surrey, who died at sea
on ship *Aurelia*, mariner. (Lands in Virginia). Probate to
Robert Bristow the younger with similar powers reserved to
brother Heneage Robinson. (Oct. 1695).Wi.

Robinson, Samuel, (of Boston, New England), who died overseas.
Probate to John Robinson with similar powers reserved to
Thomas Robinson. (Apr. 1664). Wa.

Robinson, William, of Maryland. Probate to William Calvert.
(Aug. 1697).

Robotham, George, of Talbot Co., Maryland. Limited probate to
Mary, wife of John Erp, Anne, wife of John Cooke, and Anne,
wife of William Cotton. (Nov. 1698).

Robotham, John, of ship *Dartmouth* who died at Virginia, bachelor.
Administration to next heir Richard Fuller. (Sept. 1677).

Roby, Anthony, of parts overseas, (died in Carolina). Administration with will to brother Thomas Roby; executor Andrew
Percivall now abroad and mother Early alias Avelyn Roby
having died. (July 1688). Wa.

Roche, James, of Warras Squeeke alias Warwicksweeke, Isle of
Wight, Virginia. Probate to brother Robert Roche. (Sept.
1652). Sh.Sm.

Rockwell, Honor, of Dorchester who died at Fitzhead, Somerset,
widow. (Grandchildren Richard, William and John Rockwell
in New England). Probate to son Roger Rockwell. (Jan.1638).
Wa.

Rodling, Christiana, of Virginia. Administration to husband
John Rodling. (Apr. 1676).

Rogers, Margaret, of Ipswich, New England, widow. Administration
to principal creditor William Hubbard. (Mar. 1678).

Rogers, Richard, of St. Michael Crooked Lane, London, Controller
of H.M. Mint. (Lands in Virginia). Probate to son Edward
Rogers and Jasper Draper with similar powers reserved to
daughter Anne Draper. (Sept. 1636). Wa.

Rolffe, John, of James City, Virginia. Probate to William
Peyrs. (May 1630). Sh.Wa.

Roper, Thomas, who died overseas. (Goods in Virginia). Administration with will to brother John Roper; no executor having

been named. Administration of May 1624 to Thomas Shepherd
during minority of brother and sisters on mother's side,
John, Elizabeth and Constance Shepherd, now revoked. (Feb.
1627). Wa.Wi.

Rose, John, of Deptford, Kent, who died at Virginia, bachelor.
Administration to principal creditor Robert Graves. (Nov.
1688).

Rose, Robert, of Rochester, Kent. (Brothers Christopher Rose
and Henry West in Virginia). Probate to relict Mary Rose.
(Oct. 1670). Wi.

Rounde, George, of Virginia, widower. Administration to only
sister Grissell Willmore alias Rounde. (Sept. 1654).

Rousby, Christopher, of Maryland in West Indies, widower.
Administration to brother William Rousby. (Jan. 1685).

Rowland, Peter, of Shadwell, Middlesex, who died in Virginia.
Administration to principal creditor Francis Greene; relict
Marriane Rowland renouncing. (Sept. 1674).

Rowlson, Matthew, of ship *Susanna* of London who died in Virginia,
bachelor. Administration to principal creditor Richard
Featherstone. (Aug. 1688).

Rowzee, Lewis, of Ashford, Kent, who died at Virginia. Admini-
stration to John Catlett, half brother of eldest son Ralph
Rowzee, now in Virginia, and for benefit of other children
Edward and Martha Rowzee also overseas. (July 1655).

Royse, John, of London, merchant, who died at Gravesend on
River Thames, (bound for New York). Probate to father
Daniel Royse; executor James Wancklen renouncing. (Nov.1686).

Rusher, Daniell, of Wapping, Middlesex, who died at Virginia.
Administration to relict Joane Rusher. (June 1659).

Ruske, Peter, of Virginia, bachelor. Administration to cousin
german and only next of kin Christopher Ruske. (Apr. 1656).

Ruthtra, Arthur, of Virginia. Administration to relict Anne
Ruthtra. (Sept. 1667).

Sadler, John, of St. Stephen Wallbrook, London. (Lands in
Virginia). Probate to Anthony Walker with similar powers
reserved to John Wilkey. (Jan. 1659). Wa.

Sadler, Mary, of Mayfield, Sussex, widow. (Daughter Mary Sadler
in New England). Probate to daughter Elizabeth James. (Nov.
1647). Wa.

Saffin, Thomas, of Boston, New England, who died at Stepney,
Middlesex, bachelor. Administration to Edward Hull, attorney
for father John Saffin of Boston, merchant. (Feb. 1688).

Sage, Philipp, of Stepney, Middlesex, who died in Virginia.
Administration to relict Sarah, now wife of John Rumball.
(Feb. 1691).

Saintbury alias Sainbry, Rebecca, of St. Olave, Southwark, Surrey.
(Kin in Virginia). Probate to John Spicer. (Jan. 1679). Wa.

Saker, William, of Lambeth, Surrey. (Servant Thomas Gregory
and goods in Virginia). Probate to Sir Thomas Jay and
Nathaniel Finch. (Dec. 1627). Wa.Wi.

Salter, Daniel, of ship *Seven Sisters* who died going to Virginia.
Administration to sister Avis, wife of John Nutt.

Salter, George, of Dedham, Essex. (Daughters Abigail and Hannah in New England). Probate to relict Mary Salter. (July 1654). Wa.

Salwey, Anthony, of Ann Arundell Co., Maryland. Probate to brother Richard Salwey. (Aug. 1672).

Sammes, Edward, of St. Helen the Great, London. (Cousin Stone in New England). Administration with will to relict Bennett Sammes; no executor having been named. (Feb. 1636). Sh.Wa.

Sanckley, Richard, of Virginia, bachelor. Administration to cousin George Dare. (Aug. 1675).

Sander, Francis, of Congham, Norfolk. (Kinsman Henry Spelman in Virginia). Probate to Richard Sander. (Aug. 1613). Will confirmed by sentence November 1613. Wi.

Sanford, Richard, of Virginia, bachelor. Administration to brother Francis Sanford. (May 1683).

Sayer, John, of island of Virginia. Administration to principal creditor Thomas Arnall. (Mar. 1686).

Scott, George, of London who died overseas, bachelor. (Brother Richard Scott in New England). Administration to brother Frederick Scott with will annexed; executor William Ballowe having died. (Apr. 1642). Wa.

Scott, George, of London. (Lands in Virginia). Probate to kinsman Thomas Brace. (Feb. 1649). Wa.

Scott, James, of Bristol who died at Virginia. Administration to relict Dorothy Scott. (Oct. 1698).

Scott, John, of Southampton, York Co., Long Island, New England, who died at St. Thomas, Southwark, Surrey. Limited administration with will to William Clapcott. (May 1692). Wa.

Scottow, Thomas, (surgeon of Boston, New England) who died on ship *Gerard* of London. Probate to Margaret Softly, widow. (Sept. 1699). Wa.

Scrimgeour, John, Rector of Nominie, Westmoreland Co., Virginia, bachelor. Administration to only brother William Scrimgeour. (Jan. 1693).

Scroggs, Anne, of Earls Colne, Essex, spinster. (Cousin Sarah Simmes in New England). Probate to William Harlakenden with similar powers reserved to Stephen Marshall. (Sept. 1641). Wa.

Seaman, John, of St. Dunstan in East, London, who died at Maryland. Administration to Richard Bell, guardian of only child Elizabeth Seaman; relict Elizabeth Seaman renouncing. (Apr. 1692). Revoked on production of will and probate granted by decree to relict Elizabeth Seaman. (Oct. 1692).

Searle, Joane, of Otterton, Devon, widow. (Daughters Jane Mason and Mary Veren in New England). Probate to son Richard Connant. (June 1658). Sh.

Sedgwicke, John, of St. Saviour, Southwark, Surrey. (Brother Robert Sedgwicke in New England). Probate to relict Martha Sedgwicke. (Dec. 1638). Wa.

Sellick, David, of New England, merchant. Administration to relict Susanna Tilghman alias Sellick. (Apr. 1657).

Senior, James, of Kingston upon Hull, Yorkshire, who died at Virginia, bachelor. Administration to mother Bridget Senior. (Sept. 1678).

Sergant, Stephen, of H.M.S. *Swan*, bachelor. Administration to sister Elizabeth, wife of John Davis, attorney for father Stephen Sergant in Boston, New England. Previous grant of administration with will of October ----- declared null. (Sept. 1692).

Severy, Edward, of ship *America* who died at Barbados. (Brother Andrew Severy in New England). Probate to Christian Peterson. (Oct. 1694). Wa.

Seward, John, of Bristol, merchant. (Lands at Isle of Wight, Virginia). Probate to relict Sarah Seward. (May 1651). Sh.Wi.

Sexton, Thomas, of Boston, New England, who died at Deal, Kent. Administration to principal creditor John Sturt. (June 1680).

Sharpe, John, of New England. Administration to principal creditor John Dennis. (Apr. 1667).

Sharpe, Robert, of Rappahannock River, Virginia, who died at Stepney, Middlesex. Administration to brother Abraham Sharpe. (Oct. 1666).

Sharpe, Simon, of Scathan, Lincolnshire, who died on frigate *Grantham* in America. Probate to Charles Brundon by decree. (Mar. 1659).

Sharpe, Thomas, of Virginia. Administration to principal creditor Hugh Noden. (Mar. 1678). Revoked and granted to uncle Edward Hubbert. (Apr. 1679).

Shaw, John, of Surbiton, Kingston on Thames, Surrey. (Lands in Virginia). Probate to John Heydon. (Mar. 1628). Wa.

Shawe, William, of Wapping, Middlesex, (intending for Virginia). Probate to relict Martha Shawe. (Oct. 1620). Sh.

Shaw, William, of St. Dunstan in East, London. (Brother John Shaw of New England). Probate to William Shaw and Mary Williams. (May 1693). Wa.

Sheffield, Thomas, of Virginia. Administration to nephew Lawrence Rutt during minority of son Samuel Sheffield; father William Sheffield condenting. (Aug. 1622).

Sherman, Ester, of Dedham, Essex, widow. (Kinsman Richard Sherman of New England). Probate to Bezaleel Angier. (Sept. 1646). Wa.

Sherman, Samuel, of Dedham, Essex. (Sister Bacon in New England). Probate to relict Hester Sherman and son Samuel Sherman. (Dec. 1644). Wa.

Shilborne, William, of Virginia, bachelor. Administration to mother Mary Shilborne, widow. (Feb. 1658).

Shortricke, William, of York, Old Fields, Virginia. Administration to relict Rachael, now wife of Anthony Melton. (June 1669).

Showell, Arthur, of Carolina. Administration to principal creditor John Colborne. Marked "vacat", and next entry shows Arthur Showell of Rotherhithe, Surrey, with administration to his relict Elizabeth Showell. (Apr. 1683).

Shrimpton, Edward, of Bethnal Green, Middlesex, merchant. (Children in Boston, New England). Administration with will to relict Elizabeth Shrimpton during absence overseas of brother Henry Shrimpton. (Nov. 1661). New grant March 1663. Wa.

Shurley, Ralph, of Whitechapel, Middlesex, who died at Virginia. Administration to relict Elizabeth Shurley. (Nov. 1694).

Shurt, George, of Bideford, Devon, merchant. (Brother Abraham Shurt in New England). Probate to relict Margaret Shurt. (June 1658). Sh.Wa.

Shute, Samuel, of St. Peter Cornhill, London, (Trader to New York). Probate to relict Anne Shute and son Joseph Shute with similar powers reserved to Thomas Andrews. (Dec.1685).

Sibbet, Peter, of Haddington, Scotland, who died at Virginia, bachelor. Administration to principal creditor Sibill Gray. (July 1678).

Sicklemore alias Ratcliffe, John, (of ship *Diamond* bound for Virginia) who died overseas. Probate to relict Dorothy Sicklemore with similar powers reserved to Richard Percivall. (Apr. 1611). Sh.Wi.

Silvester, Constant, of Brampton, Huntingdonshire. (Lands in New England). Probate to relict Grace Silvester. (Oct 1671).

Revoked and administration granted to daughter Grace, wife
of Sir Henry Pickering. (June 1702). Wa.

Simondson, Peter, of ship *Merchants Adventure*. Administration
to Susan, wife and attorney of next heir Michael Deane in
Virginia. (Dec. 1696).

Simpson, John, of Stepney, Middlesex, who died at Virginia.
Administration to principal creditor Abraham Barret; relict
Elizabeth Simpson renouncing. (June 1683). Inventory PROB
4/1138.

Simson, Martin, of Hackney, Middlesex. (Niece Hester Simson
in New England). Probate to Henry Ashurst, ------ Blackmore
and Thomas Gellibrand. (Aug. 1665). Wa.

Sinckler, John, of ship *Owners Adventure* who died in Virginia,
widower. Probate to Anne Hill. (July 1697).

Skilton, Mary, of St. Mary Woolnoth, London. (Sister Joane,
wife of John Wilkinson in New England). Probate to nephew
Isaac Ashe. (Jan. 1654). Wa.

Slany, Thomas, of Kings Lynn, Norfolk. (Daughter Joane Kinge
in New England). Probate to Thomas Linge and Thomas Moore.
(June 1649). Wa.

Slaughter, Elizabeth, of Bristol Diocese. (Reference to Isaac
Walker in New England). Administration with will to Robert
Culme; no executor having been named. (June 1646). Wa.

Smallay, Captain Robert, of Bermuda Hundred, Virginia. Administration with will to relict Elizabeth Smallay; executor
Samuel Argall renouncing. (Nov. 1621). Sh.Sm.Wi.

Smith, Elizabeth, of Taunton, Somerset, widow. (Bequest to
Jane, wife of William Williams of New England). Probate to
Johan Westoner. (July 1654). Wa.

Smith, Henry, of London. (Nephew Henry Mundy in New England).
Probate to Richard Berridge. (May 1653). Sh.Wa.

Smith, Henry, of Watford, Hertfordshire. (Brother William Smith
in Virginia). Probate to relict Sarah Smith. (Feb. 1666).
Wi.

Smith, Henry, of Wraysbury, Buckinghamshire. (Daughter Mary
Lord in New England). Probate to relict Anne Smith. (Oct.
1682). Wa.

Smith, Jehosaphat, of London, who died at Boston, New England.
Probate to brother James (?Jacob) Smith. (July 1678).

Smith, John, of Southwold, Suffolk. (Goods in New England).
Probate to relict Helen Smith. (Feb. 1651). Sh.Wa.

Smith, John, citizen and merchant tailor of London. (Cousin
William Smith in New England). Probate to daughter Sarah
Whiting). (Oct. 1656). Wa.

Smith, John, citizen and cook of London. (Bequest to Allen
Whore in Virginia). Probate to son William Smith; son-in-
law George Pouchin renouncing. (July 1672). Wi.

Smith, John, of Carolina. Administration to principal creditor
John Colborne. (Apr. 1683).

Smith, John, of Pennsylvania. Administration to William Wright,
attorney for relict Jane Smith in Scotland. (Feb. 1689).

Smith, John, of Boston, New England, who died on ship *Nonsuch*.
Administration to Elisha Cartwright, attorney for relict Mary
Smith in New England. (July 1698).

Smith, Nathaniel, who died overseas. (Sister Hannah Mellowes
in New England). Administration with will to kinsman
Thomas Edwards and cousin Nathaniel Edwards; no executor
having been named. (Mar. 1651). Sh.Wa.

Smith, Oliver, of Ratcliffe, Stepney, Middlesex, who died at
Virginia on ship *Susanna*. Probate to relict Mary Smith.
(Oct. 1686).

Smith, Phebe, of Virginia, spinster. Administration to cousin and next of kin Richard Crowder. (Oct. 1676).

Smith, Richard, of ship *Duke of York* who died at Virginia or at sea, bachelor. Probate to Elizabeth Davis. (June 1680).

Smith, Robert, of St. Michael Bassishaw, London. (Lands in Virginia). Probate to relict Judith Smith. (July 1623). Revoked on her death and administration granted to James Clarke, half brother of daughter Hannah Smith during her minority. (Feb. 1630). Wa.

Smith, Roger, of Virginia. Administration to sisters Gertrude and Audrey James alias Smith. (Oct. 1625).

Smith, Simon, of Stepney, Middlesex. (Granddaughter Judith, wife of Richard Toozer of New England). Probate to Simon Smith. (Jan. 1666). Wa.

Smith, Thomas, of West Clandon, Surrey. (Brother John Smith in New England). Probate to nephew Jeremy Smith. (Oct. 1651). Wa.

Smith, Warrin, of Holborn, Middlesex. (Adventurer in Virginia). Probate to Dennis Breton. (May 1615). Wi.

Smith, William, of St. John Baptist, Bristol, who died at Virginia. Administration to relict Margaret Smith. (Nov. 1679).

Smithett, Robert, of Bermondsey, Surrey, late of H.M.S. *Humber* and *Newport* who died at Boston, New England. Probate to relict Proteza Smithett. (Oct. 1695).

Snape, Timothy, (of London, bound for Virginia) who died overseas, bachelor. Probate to brother Samuel Snape and sister Hannah Barker alias Snape. (July 1629). Wa.

Snell, Nathaniel, of Hillingdon, Middlesex. (Bequest to David Maybanke in Carolina). Probate to relict Sarah Snell. (Apr. 1692). Wa.

Snooke, John, of St. Clement Danes, London. (Lands in Virginia). Probate to Ralph Sedgewicke with similar powers reserved to William Higginson. (Sept. 1665). Wa.

Somers, Sir George, of Barne, Dorset, (bound for Virginia). Probate to brother John Somers. (Aug. 1611). Sh.Wa.

Somers, John, of Virginia, bachelor. Administration to mother Agnes Somers. (Nov. 1672).

Southcot, Leonard, of ship *Loyal Rebecca* who died at sea, (in Virginia). Probate to Thomas Short. (June 1677).

Southell, Seth, of Virginia. Administration with will to principal creditor William Bowtell; relict Anne Southell having died before executing. (Feb. 1697).

Southen, George, of Virginia. Administration to relict Elizabeth Southen. (Nov. 1673).

Souther, Nathaniel, of ship *Samuel and Henry*, bachelor. Administration to brother Samuel Souther, attorney for father Joseph Souther in Boston, New England. (Aug. 1691).

Sparhawke, John the elder, of Great Coggeshall, Essex. (Brother Sparhawke in New England). Probate to son John Sparhawke and Christopher Sheriffe. (Sept. 1653). Wa.

Sparke, Michael, of St. Sepulchre without Newgate, London. (Goods in Virginia). Probate to son-in-law Humphrey Baskervile. (Mar. 1654). Wi.

Spelman, Thomas, of Truro, Cornwall, (and Virginia). Administration with will to brother Francis Spelman during absence overseas of relict Hannah Spelman. (Apr. 1627). Sentence for validity of will December 1628. Sh.Wa.

Spencer, Thomas, of Kingston on Thames, Surrey. (Goods in New England). Probate to Nicholas Kidwell. (Aug. 1648). Wa.

Spencer, William, of Cople, Bedfordshire. (Brother Nicholas Spencer of Virginia). Probate to John Luke with similar power reserved to Oliver Luke. (June 1686). Wa.

Stacie, Thomas, of Maidstone, Kent. (Lands in Virginia).
Probate to Robert Joye. (Sept. 1619). Wi.
Stanesby, John, of Maryland, ?widower. Administration to
brother William Stanesby. (Jan. 1692).
Stanford, Hugh, of Virginia, bachelor. Administration to
brother Anthony Stanford. (July 1658).
Stanley, Hugh, of Maryland. Administration with will to
Elizabeth Stanley, mother of nephews John and Edward
Stanley during their minority; relict Dorothy Stanley
renouncing. (Dec. 1671).
Stanton, George, of Virginia. Administration to Catherine
Cooke, widow, grandmother of children Joseph and Mary
Stanton during their minority. (Aug. 1698). Further
grant May 1699
Stanton, Nicholas, of Ipswich, Suffolk, clerk. (Kinsmen
Judith, wife of Henry Smith, and Joseph Moyse in New
England). Probate to relict Mary Stanton. (Feb. 1650). Wa.
Stedman, Solomon, of Boston, New England. Administration with
will to Henry Cole, trustee for executor John Stedman now
overseas. (Dec. 1697). Wa.
Steele, John, of London, (who died in Zeeland on return from
Virginia). Probate to relict Amy Steele. (Dec. 1638).
Sh.Wi.
Stegge (Stagg), Captain Thomas, of Virginia, who died off the
coast there. Probate to relict Elizabeth Stagg. (July 1652).
Sh.Wa.
Stegge, Thomas, of Virginia. Probate to relict Sarah Stegge.
(May 1671). Wa.
Stent, William, of Portsmouth, Hampshire, who died at Virginia
on ship *Planters Adventure*, bachelor. Administration to
brother Richard Stent; mother Grace Cooke alias Stent
renouncing. (Apr. 1680).
Stevens, Edward, of Bristol who died at Virginia. Administra-
tion to relict Grace Stevens. (Apr. 1694).
Stevens, Nathaniel, of St. Merrin, Cornwall, who died at Virginia on ship *Margarett*. Administration to William Peter,
attorney for relict Anne Stephens *(sic)* now in distant
parts. (June 1679).
Stevens, William, of Virginia. Administration to principal
creditor Thomas Jauncey. (Sept. 1651).
Stephens, William, of Bristol, who died at Virginia. Administration to relict Alice Stephens. (July 1684).
Stepkin, Charles the elder, of London who died at Virginia.
Administration with will to Elizabeth Stepkin, widow,
mother of children Charles and Theodosia Stepkin during
their minority; executors Joseph Lowe and George Richards
renouncing. (July 1689).
Sterry, William, of Bristol who died at Boston, New England.
Administration with will to principal creditor Giles Merricke;
executor Adam Winthropp in Boston and relict Charity Sterry
renouncing. (Oct. 1685).
Stevens - see Stephens.
Steward, William, of Deptford, Kent, who died on H.M.S. *Deptford*
at Boston, New England. Administration to relict Sarah
Steward. (July 1698).
Stiffe, William, of Upton, Essex, who died on ship *Rainbow*,
bachelor. (Trader to Virginia). Administration to cousin
and next of kin John Digby. (Oct. 1673).
Stocker, Joseph, of Wiviliscombe, Somerset. (Son Ephraim Stocker
went to Virginia). Probate to Mary Stocker, relict. (May
1679). Revoked on her death and administration granted to
Amos Stocker, Robert Hayne, Thomas Grove and Nicholas

Marshall, guardians of children Mary, Ephraim and Obadiah
Stocker at Wiviliscombe during their minority. (Feb. 1681).
See NGSQ 67/212.

Stockman, William, of Barford, Wiltshire. (Cousin Gerret
Edington in Virginia). Probate to brother Joseph Stockman.
(Oct. 1658). Wi.

Stolpys alias Stolpee, John, of Virginia who died on ship
Mary. Probate to Albert Albertson. (Apr. 1692).

Stolion, Jane, of London, widow, who died overseas. (Goods in
New England). Probate to son Abraham Stolion. (May 1647).
Sh.Wa.

Stolyon, Thomas, of Warbleton, Sussex. (Goods in New England).
Administration with will, after sentence for validity, to
Samuel Spatchurst, John Wood the elder and Samuel Store,
attornies for the people of Warbleton; executors Richard
Weller and Edward Hawkesworth renouncing. (Nov. 1680). Wa.

Stone, Margaret, of St. Peter le Poor, London, widow. (Husband
William Stone in Virginia). Probate to Joseph Godwin.
(Nov. 1676).

Story, George, of Stepney, Middlesex, who died at Virginia.
Administration to relict Elizabeth Story. (Aug. 1675).

Storey, Ralph, of Wapping, Middlesex, who died at Virginia.
Probate to relict Avice Storey. (June 1664).

Strachey, William, of St. Augustine, London. (Daughter Arabella,
wife of John Waters in Virginia). Probate to George Richards.
(Mar. 1687).

Stratton, John, of James City, Virginia. Administration to
relict Joanna Stratton. (June 1641).

Stringer, Rowland, of Plymouth, Devon, who died at Virginia on
ship *Daniel and Elizabeth*, bachelor. Administration to
father Francis Stringer. (Mar. 1690).

Sturges, Henry, of ship *John and Margarett* who died at Maryland.
Administration to principal creditor Adam Mason; relict
Mary Sturges renouncing. (Aug. 1697).

Sturman, Richard, of Nomany, Westmoreland, Virginia. Probate
to Rebecca Frodsham alias Sturman. (Sept. 1672). Wa.

Style, John, of Stepney, Middlesex. (Nephew George Burrough
of New England, clerk). Probate to William Burrough.
(July & Aug. 1686). Wa.

Style, Samuel, of Portugal. (Sister Elizabeth Style in New
England). Probate to Henry Boade with similar powers reserved to Simon Smith and John Middleton. (Apr. 1665). Wa.

Sutton, John, of St. Giles Cripplegate, London, who died in
Virginia. Administration to relict Frances Sutton. (May
1651).

Swan, Thomas, of Southwark, Surrey, who died in Virginia.
Administration to Micajah Perry, attorney for relict Mary,
now wife of Robert Randall in Virginia. (Oct. 1691).

Swett, Joseph, (of Boston, New England), who died on H.M.S.
Defiant. Probate to John Gill. (Jan. 1696).

Swift, James, of St. Mary Abchurch, London, who died at Hackney,
Middlesex. (Goods in Boston, New England). Probate to
relict Sarah Swift. (June 1684).

Sybada, Kempo, of Stepney, Middlesex, mariner. (Lands in New
England). Probate to relict Mary Sybada. (Apr. 1659). Wa.

Sykes, Bernard, of London who died in Virginia. Administration
by decree to George Gay during absence overseas of relict
Elizabeth Sykes. (May 1682).

Symonds, John, of Great Yeldham, Essex. (Cousin William Symonds
in New England). Probate to Jane Symonds, John Pepys and
Thomazine Pepys. (May 1693). Wa.

Tatton, William, of St. Mary Aldermary, London. (Bequest to
John Machen in Virginia). Probate to son William Tatton.
(Feb. 1666). Further grant July 1682. Wa.
Taverner, Robert, of Maryland, bachelor. Administration to
brother Thomas Taverner. (Feb. 1676).
Tavernor, Robert, of London who died in Virginia, merchant.
Probate, after sentence for validity of will, to Bridget
Fowlkes. (Jan. 1677).
Tayloe, William, of Virginia. Administration to brother Thomas
Tayloe. (Aug. 1661).
Taylor, Daniel, of St. Stephen, Coleman Street, London. (Brother
Edward Rawson in New England). Probate to Mark Hildersley
the elder, late Alderman of London. (Apr. 1655). Wa.
Taylor, Daniel, of St. Martin Ludgate, London, who died in
Maryland. Administration to sister and next of kin Anne
Yates alias Taylor. (July 1677).
Taylor, Henry, of St. Margaret, Westminster, Middlesex, who
died in Virginia. Administration to relict John (sic)
Taylor. (May 1677).
Taylor, John, of Whitechapel, Middlesex, who died in Virginia.
Administration to Cicely, wife of principal creditor Alexan-
der Nash during his absence. (June 1665).
Taylor, John, of Knightsbridge, Middlesex. (Son Samuel Taylor
in Virginia). Probate to Thomas Grover and Nicholas Broad-
way. (May 1641). Wi.
Taylor, Robert, of Stepney, Middlesex, who died in Virginia.
Administration to relict Sarah, now wife of John Bidmore.
(Oct. 1656).
Teare, Samuel, of ship *Anne* who died at Virginia. Administra-
tion to relict Mary Teare. (July 1695).
Terrell, Robert, of London, merchant. (Goods in Virginia).
Probate to cousin Robert Alpen. (Nov. 1677). Wi.
Tew, Richard, of Newport, Rhode Island. Probate to brother
John Tew with powers reserved to son Henry Tew. (Mar. 1674).
Wa.
Thatcher, Peter, of New Sarum, Wiltshire, clerk. (Brother
Anthony Thatcher in New England). Probate to relict Alice
Thatcher. (Aug. 1641). Wa.
Thomas, Bartholomew, of Virginia. Administration to relict
Mary Thomas. (Nov. 1673).
Thomas, William, (of Virginia), who died at sea. Probate to
relict Judith Thomas. (Oct. 1660). Wi.
Thompson, Christopher, of island of Virginia, widower. Admini-
stration to principal creditor John Andrewes. (Sept. 1687).
Thompson, David, of Stepney, Middlesex, who died at Virginia on
ship *Willing Minde*. Administration to creditor Nicholas
Felton; relict Mary Thompson renouncing. (June 1679).
Thompson, Henry, of Boston, New England. Administration to
John Sharpe, attorney for relict Elizabeth Thompson in New
England. (Dec. 1686).
Tompson, Jacob, of Bristol who died (at Virginia) on ship *Sarah*
of Bristol. Probate to relict Susanna Tompson; no executor
having been named. (Aug. 1699).
Thompson, John, of Virginia. Probate to Thomas Haistwell with
similar powers reserved to Henry Hartwell. (Apr. 1699). Wi.
Thompson, Maurice, of Haversham, Buckinghamshire. (Lands in
Virginia). Probate to son Sir John Thompson. (May 1676). Wa.
Thomson, Robert, of Stoke Newington, Middlesex. (Lands in New
England). Probate to son Joseph Thomson with similar powers
reserved to relict Frances Thomson. (Dec. 1694). Validity
of will confirmed Trinity 1695. Wa.

Thompson, Samuel, of St. Gregory, London. (Nephew Thomas
Thompson to go to his mother in New England). Probate to
Samuel Gelibrand. (Nov. 1668). Wa.
Thomson, Samuel, of Shadwell, Middlesex, who died in Virginia.
Probate to Thomas Anderson. (June 1694).
Thorndike, Herbert, Prebend of Westminster. (Nieces Alice and
Martha Thorndike of New England). Probate to Edward Buckley.
(July 1672). Wa.
Thorowgood, Joseph, of London who died at Carolina, bachelor.
Probate to John Ashby with similar powers reserved to
brother William Thorowgood. (Jan. 1685). Wa.
Thorpe. Catherine, of Middle Plantation, York Co., (?Virginia),
widow. Administration to father Francis Seyton. (Nov.1695).
Thorpe, Otho, of All Hallows on Wall, London. (Cousin John
Grice in Virginia). Probate to relict Frances Thorpe.
(July 1686). Wi.
Thrasher, William, of ship *Success* who died at sea, widower.
Administration to sister Mary Hill, wife of William Thrasher
(sic) now living in (*New*) England. (Aug. 1680).
Throckmorton, Raphael, of St. Gregory, London. (Brother-in-law
William Wallthall in Virginia). Probate to Edward Throck-
morton. (May 1670).
Throckmorton, Robert, of Paxton Parva, Huntingdonshire. (Lands
in Virginia). Probate to Thomas Bromsall and Edward Mason.
(May 1699).
Thurmur, John, of Calvert Co., Maryland. Administration with
will to principal creditor Thomas Elwes; no executor having
been named. (Feb. 1669).
Thurston, Robert, of St. Sepulchre, London, (bound to Virginia).
Probate to brother-in-law Thomas Wilde. (Jan. 1678). Wi.
Tice, William, who died overseas, bachelor. (Sister Anne Tice
in New England). Probate to Robert Smith with similar powers
reserved to John Crouch and William Horder. (Aug. 1649).
Sh.Wa.
Tilden, Joseph, citizen and girdler of London. (Nieces in New
England). Administration with will to brother Hopestill
Tilden during absence of nephew Joseph Tilden, son of
brother Nathaniel Tilden. (Mar. 1643).
Todd, Thomas the elder, of Baltimore, Maryland. Special admini-
stration with will to son Thomas Todd. (Mar. 1678).
Tomlins, Thomas, of St. Bartholomew the Great, London. (Lands
in Virginia). Probate to Francis Camfield. (Sept. 1666).
Wa.Wi.
Toms, William, of Topsham, Devon, who died at Virginia, bachelor.
Administration with will to Elizabeth Evans, wife of executor
Richard Evans during his absence overseas. (July 1681).
Tonstall, John, of Maryland, bachelor. Administration to brother
Thomas Tonstall. (May 1685).
Tonte, Robert, of St. Olave, Southwark, Surrey, who died in
Virginia on ship *Dunbarton*, mariner. Administration to
principal creditor John Jordan. (June 1688).
Tookey, Job, of H.M.S. *Newport*, bachelor. Administration with
will to Henry Fitzhugh, brother and attorney of executor
Robert Fitzhugh at Boston, New England. (Dec. 1696).
Topping, Richard, of Solbery, Buckinghamshire. (Children in
New England). Probate to relict Alice Topping. (Apr. 1658).
Sh.Wa.
Topping, Samuel, of Stepney, Middlesex. (Lands in Virginia).
Probate to relict Hannah Topping. (May 1693).
Torkington, Joseph, of Virginia. Probate to brother Samuel
Torkington. (Apr. 1653). Sh.Wi.

Toulson, John, of Ackamack, Virginia, bachelor. Administration
to brother William Toulson. (Sept. 1656).

Tovey, Nicholas, of Maryland. Probate to relict Anne Tovey.
(June 1675).

Townsend, Joane - see Michell.

Townsend, Mary, of Newton or Higham Ferrers, Northamptonshire,
who died at Virginia, widow. Administration to principal
creditors Walter and John Jeffreys. (Nov. 1694).

Traherne, William, of St. Clement Danes, Middlesex. (Brother
Michael Traherne in Virginia). Probate to Henry Haisman
with similar powers reserved to Ellen Haisman. (June 1658).
Sh.Wa.

Trent, James, of ship *Charles* in King's service, (in Pennsylvania). Probate to Thomas Coutts. (Apr. 1699). Revoked
and granted to brother William Trent. (Nov. 1699).

Trew, Henry, of Limehouse, Middlesex, who died in Virginia.
Administration to relict Susanna Trew. (May 1661).

Trotman, Throckmorton, of St. Giles Cripplegate, London.
(Cousin in Virginia). Probate to Samuel and Edward Trotman.
(Oct. 1664). Wi.

Trumball, Samuel, who died on ship *Elizabeth* going to Virginia.
Administration to relict Elizabeth Trumball. (July 1659).

Trye, Elianor, of St. Lawrence Jewry, London, spinster.
(Nephew Thomas Buckley in New England). Probate to Susan
and John Viccaridge. (Mar. 1692). Wa.

Tull, Richard, of Maryland, bachelor. Administration to principal creditor Daniel Biddle. (July 1692). Revoked on
production of will and probate granted to said Daniel Biddle;
Henry Medlicott, John Ewer and Jane Peck renouncing. (Oct.
1699).

Turpin, James, of Virginia, widower. Probate to John Smith.
(May 1678).

Tuttie, John, of St. Bartholomew by Exchange, London, citizen
and fruiterer or London. (Sister Hannah Knight of New
England). Probate to relict Rachel Tuttie. (Oct. 1657).

Tyler, Grace, wife of John Tyler of Colchester, Essex. (Sister
Elizabeth Brock of Dedham, New England). Probate to William
Young with similar powers reserved to John Browne. (July
1647). Sh.Wa.

Upington, Walter, of Bristol who died at Maryland. Probate to
George Tite and Roger Bagg. (Sept. 1692).

Vansoldt, Elizabeth, of St. Botolph Bishopsgate, London, widow.
(Son Abraham Vansoldt in Virginia). Administration with
will to daughter Ann White; executor James White having
died. (Oct. 1665). Wi.Wa.

Vassall, William, of Barbados. (Lands in New England).
Probate to son John Vassall. (June 1657). Wa.

Vaughan alias Jones, Jane, of Kent Co., Maryland. Administration to father Henry Jones and husband Charles Vaughan.
(July 1681).

Vernon, Margery, of St. Martin Ludgate, London, widow. (Son-
in-law Francis Vernon in New England). Probate to Robert
Potter and Mary Vernon. (May 1656). Wa.

Viggory, Thomas, of New England who died at Deptford, Kent,
bachelor. Administration to Elizabeth Jacobson, wife and
attorney of John Jacobson during his absence. (Nov. 1690).

Vincent, Elizabeth, of Holborn, Middlesex, widow. (Kinswoman
Love Meredith in Virginia). Probate to Benjamin Wyche.
(Nov. 1660). Wi.

Vizer, Ralph, formerly of Dublin, Ireland, but late of Bristol.
(Son Henry Vizer in Virginia). Probate to relict Bridget
Vizer. (Sept. 1667). Wi.

Wade, Joseph, (of Boston, New England), who died on ship *Mary*.
Probate to George Golden with similar powers reserved to
Thomas Linch, Valentine Baker and William Barton. (Oct.
1692). Wa.

Wade alias Atkins, Mary, of Maryland. Administration to sister
Sarah Starkey alias Atkins, wife of John Starkey. (Dec.1660).

Wade, William, of Westham, Sussex, who died overseas, (bound
to Pennsylvania), bachelor. Probate to Philip Ford.
(Oct. 1682). Wa.

Wayte, John, of Worcester. (Lands in Pennsylvania). Probate
to relict Elizabeth Wayte. (Nov. 1691).

Waite, William, of Stepney, Middlesex, who died at Virginia.
Administration to principal creditor Edmund Cussey; relict
Dorothy Waite renouncing. (Nov. 1671).

Walker, Bartholomew, of ship *Robert and William* who died in
Virginia on King's service, bachelor. Administration to
mother Frances Walker. (Sept. 1678).

Walker, Daniel, of Woodbridge, Suffolk, who died at Virginia.
Administration to principal creditor Edward Dakins; relict
Susan Walker renouncing. (May 1672). Inventory PROB4/6669.

Walker, Hannah, of St. Giles Cripplegate, London, widow. (Son
Thomas Walker of New England). Probate to John Jackson.
(Nov. 1675). Further grant December 1700. Wa.

Walker, Joseph, of Westminster, Middlesex. (Lands in Virginia).
Probate to Mary Snow. (Feb. 1667). Wa.

Wall, Bartholomew, of Blakenham on the Waters, Suffolk.
(Daughter Anna Jacob in New England). Probate to daughter
Mary Wall. (Apr. 1673). Wa.

Wallin alias Poulter, Hannah, of St. Andrew Undershaft, London,
spinster. (Kinsman Thomas Poulter in Virginia). Probate
to Joseph Alston. (Aug. 1663).

Walter, John, of New England, bachelor. Administration to
cousin and next of kin William Walter. (Jan. 1697).

Walter, Richard, of New England. Administration with will to
relict Sarah Walter; no executor having been named. (Feb.
1654). Revoked and her death and granted to her husband
and administrator Thomas Luck. (Feb. 1661). Sh.

Walton alias Wanton, Robert, of Virginia. Administration to
principal creditor John Tayloe; relict Elizabeth Walton
alias Wanton renouncing. (June 1670).

Walton, Walter, son of John Walton of Spofforth, Yorkshire.
(Interests in Virginia and Maryland). Probate to Richard
Lawson with similar powers reserved to Alexander Ewes.
(Aug. 1650). Sh.Wi.

Wampers, John - see White.

Wanton, Robert - see Walton.

Ward, Henry, of Stepney, Middlesex, who died at Virginia.
Administration to relict Sarah Ward. (June 1659).

Ware, John, of Boston, New England, who died at sea on ship
Friendship. Limited administration to John Hill of St.
Catherine Coleman, London, merchant, attorney for relict
Sarah Ware in Boston. (July 1694). Revoked and granted
to Sarah Garland alias Ware, the relict, now wife of Thomas
Garland and now in England. (Feb. 1697).

Warkman, Mark - see Glocester.

Warner, John, of Stepney, Middlesex, (mariner, with goods in
Virginia). Administration to relict Frances Warner. (Dec.
1677).

Warnett, Thomas, of James City, Virginia, mariner. Probate to
relict Thomazine Warnett. (Nov. 1630). Sh.Sm.Wa.

Warnsley, John, of St. Olave, Southwark, Surrey, (bound for
Virginia). Probate to William Glassbrooke. (May 1698). Wi.

Washington, Laurence, of Luton, Bedfordshire, who died at
Virginia. Administration to principal creditor Edmund Jones.
(May 1677).

Waters, Edward, of Elizabeth City, Virginia, who died at
Hormead, Hertfordshire. Administration with will to brother
John Waters during minority of son William Waters. (Sept.
1630). Sh.

Watkin, Gifford, who died in Virginia, bachelor. Probate to
brother Arthur Watkin. (June 1637). Sh.

Watkins, Christopher, of St. Botolph Aldersgate, London.
(Kinsman George Watkins of Virginia). Administration to
relict Jane Watkins. (Dec. 1673).

Watson, John, of Shadwell, Middlesex, who died at Virginia,
widower. Administration to principal creditor Edward
Savage. (May 1677).

Watson, Philip, of New England, widower. Administration to
son Elia Watson. (Aug. 1697).

Watson, Richard, of St. Margaret, Westminster, Middlesex.
(Stepson Robert Boodle of Virginia). Probate to ?Bruce
Clench. (Jan. 1686). Further grant September 1733. Wa.

Watson, William, of Rotherhithe, Surrey, who died at sea near
island of Carolina. Administration to principal creditor
Thomas Balden. (Sept. 1686).

Watson, William, citizen and blacksmith of London. (Daughter
Rebecca in New England). Probate to Edward Palmer and
Thomas Rollinson. (Oct. 1652). Sh.

Watson, William, who died on ship *James Towne* bound to Virginia,
mariner. Administration to relict Sarah Watson. (Aug. 1659).

Watts, Cornelius, of Wells, Somerset. (Kinsman William Watts
in Virginia). Probate to relict Ann Watts and children
Edmund and Ann Watts. (Oct. 1640). Wi.

Watts, Edward, of Stepney, Middlesex, who died in Virginia. Administration to principal creditor John Bugbye; relict Jane Watts renouncing. (July 1669).

Waugh, David, of Stafford Co., Virginia, who died on ship *Elizabeth*. Administration with will to Henry Bowen, attorney for brother Peter Waugh overseas. (Feb. 1694). Wi.

Way, George, of Dorchester, Dorset. (Lands in New England). Probate to relict Sarah Way. (Dec. 1641). Wa.

Wayte - see Waite.

Weare, Thomas, of Charfield, Gloucestershire. (Brother Peter Weare of York, New England). Probate to brother Peter Weare. (Oct. 1685).

Webb, Robert, of Virginia, bachelor. Administration to cousin german William Webb; uncle William Webb renouncing. (Aug. 1659).

Webster, John, of Maryland in Virginia, bachelor. Administration to brother Robert Webster. (Nov. 1671).

Weedon, John, of Boston, New England, who died on H.M.S. *Mary*. Administration to Thomas Dummer, attorney for relict Ruth Weedon overseas. (July 1699).

Weedon, William, of St. Botolph Bishopsgate, London. (Nephew and niece William and Ann Weedon of Maryland). Probate to William Weedon; Anne Weedon being dead. (Nov. 1692).

Wells, Richard, who died overseas (Maryland). Probate to Richard Wells. (Nov. 1668). Wa.

West, Francis, of Winchester, Hampshire, who died in Virginia. Probate to relict Jane West. (Apr. 1634). Sh.Wi.

West, John, (formerly of New York, late of Boston) who died at St. Martin Ludgate, London. Probate to relict Anne West. (Nov. 1691). Wa.

West, John, of St. Sepulchre, London. (Grandson John East and daughter Hannah Streete in Pennsylvania). Probate to son Richard West. (July 1699).

West, William, of Slinfold, Sussex, (bound for Virginia). Probate to Mary Blount. (June 1616). Sh.Wi.

West, William, of Eaton, Buckinghamshire. (Son William West of Virginia). Probate to Thomas West. (June 1687). Wa.

Westhrope, John, of London, merchant, who died in Virginia. Probate to Edward Henshaw and Edmond Beckford. (June 1656). Revoked and granted to sister Dorothy Drewers alias Westhrope. (Oct. 1660). Sh.Wi.

Westlake, Edward, of Maryland. Administration to Ellis Asby, brother of relict Margery Westlake in Maryland. (May 1694).

Whaplett, Thomas, who died in Virginia. Probate to sister Rebecca Whaplett with similar powers reserved to John Redman. (July 1636). Revoked on death of Rebecca Whaplett and administration granted to Ralph Gregge. (Nov. 1636). Sh.Wi.

Wharton, Edmund, of New England, bachelor. Administration to brother George Wharton. (June 1678).

Wharton, Richard, of Boston, New England, merchant. Probate to Samuel Read and Nathaniel Whitfield after sentence for validity of will with similar powers reserved to Waite Winthrop, John Eyres, John Higginson and Isaac Addington. (Apr. 1690).

Whearley, Henry, of Barbados. (Brother Francis Whearley in Pennsylvania). Probate to brother Daniel Whearley. (Apr. 1689).

Wheeler, Francis, of London, merchant, (bound to Virginia). Probate to son Francis Wheeler. (Mar. 1660).

Wheeler, James, of Maryland, bachelor. Administration to sister Alice Gutridge alias Wheeler. (Oct. 1674).

Wheeler, Richard, citizen and innholder of London. (Grand-
children Richard and John Moye in Virginia). Probate to
George Kelsey. (Jan. 1658). Sh.Wi.
Whilhelme, Christian, of St. Olave, Southwark, Surrey, galley
pot maker. (Adventurer in Virginia). Probate to daughter
Mary and her husband Thomas Townsend. (Apr. 1630). Wi.
White, Edmund, of St. Giles Cripplegate, London. (Son-in-law
Humphrey Davie of Boston, New England). Probate to son
Edmund White and William Coxe. (Dec. 1674). Wa.
White, James, who died overseas (at Boston, New England).
Probate to William White with similar powers reserved to
Henry Hawley, Edward Pye, James Beake, William Bate and
Jeremy Edgington. (Feb. 1668).
White, James, who died in Virginia on ship *Archangel*, bachelor.
Administration to principal creditor John Barnes. (Apr.
1694).
White, John, vicar of Cheriton, Wiltshire. (Nephews in Vir-
ginia). Probate to John Broadhurst and Phillis Broadhurst.
(Feb. 1672). Wi.
White alias Wampers, John, of Boston, New England, who died while
travelling in Stepney, Middlesex. Probate to John Blake with
similar powers reserved to Edward Pratt. (Oct. 1679). Wa.
White, William, of London who died overseas. (Lands in Vir-
ginia). Probate to brother John White. (June 1627). Wa.
White, William, of St. Bride, London. (Brother John White in
Virginia). Probate to children William White and Elizabeth
Saunders. (Dec. 1676). Wi.
White, William, of James City, Virginia. Limited administration
to Micajah Perry, attorney for relict Jane White during her
absence. (Aug. 1682).
White, William, of H.M.S. *St. Albans'* prize, drowned in Virginia.
Probate to Edward Daniel. (Sept. 1697).
Whitehaire, Robert, of Willesden, Middlesex, who died in Vir-
ginia. Administration to relict Elizabeth Whitehaire.
(June 1674).
Whitehead, Mary, of Binfield, Berkshire. (Son Richard Whitehead
in Virginia). Probate to daughter Philadelphia Whitehead.
(May 1679).
Whitehead, Richard, of Windsor on Connecticut River, who died
at St. Mary's, Warwick. Probate to John Andrewes with
similar powers reserved to Thomas Fish. (June 1645). Sh.Wa.
Whiting, John, of Hadleigh, Suffolk. (Brother Robert Payne in
New England). Probate to relict Judith Whiting. (Jan.1645).
Wa.
Whiting, Simon, of Dedham, Essex. (Bequest to Richard Sherman
of New England). Probate to relict Jane Whiting; Clement
Fenn renouncing. (June 1637). Wa.
Whitlock, Thomas, of Virginia, bachelor. Administration to
nephew and next of kin Anthony Whitlock. (July 1680).
Whitmore, Benjamin, (of Middletown, New England) who died on
H.M.S. *Royal Katherine*. Administration with will to
Isabella Edwards, wife of Hugh Edwards, attorney for execu-
tor Charles Hill. (Sept. 1696).
Whittacre, George, (passenger from Virginia to London).
Probate of nuncupative will to William Scott. (June 1654).
Sh.Wa.
Whittingham, William, formerly of Boston, New England, who died
at St. Mary Savoy, Middlesex. Probate to Nathaniel Hubbard
with similar powers reserved to John Lawrence, William
Hubert and John Lewen. (Apr. 1672). Double probate to
William Hubbert with similar powers reserved to John
Lawrence and John Lewin. (Mar. 1678). Wa.

Wickes, Robert, of Staines, Middlesex. (Son John Wickes in
New England). Probate to son Thomas Wickes. (Nov. 1638).
Wa.

Wilcocks, Captain John, of Plymouth, Devon, (and Accomack,
New England). Probate to relict Temperance Wilcocks. (June
1628). Sh.Wa.

Wilkinson, Henry, of Nottingham. (Cousin Isabel Blood in New
England). Administration with will to Richard Hardmett).
Mar. 1646). Wa.

Willdy, Benjamin, of Carolina. Probate to sister Martha, wife
of Edward Wood; mother Martha Doggett having died in
testator's lifetime. (Feb. 1697).

Williams, Benjamin, of Stoke near Guildford, Surrey. (Cousins
Samuel, Thomas and Benjamin Williams and Elizabeth Bird in
New England). Probate to brother Nathaniel Williams.
(Sept. 1698). Wa.

Williams, Jane, of Whetenhurst, Gloucestershire, spinster.
Brother and sister Richard and Elizabeth Williams in New
England). Probate to brother-in-law John Hall. (June 1655).
Wa.

Williams, Richard, of St. Catherine Creechurch, London, bound
to Virginia, bachelor. Probate to Walter Hawkins. (May
1653). Wi.

Williams, Richard, of Limehouse, Middlesex, who died at Virginia, widower. Administration to Susan Stock, aunt of
children Richard, Jone, Anne, Mary and Stephen Williams
during their minority. (July 1655).

Williamson, Richard, of St. Andrew Undershaft, London, citizen
and merchant tailor of London. (Brother Roger Williamson
of Virginia). Probate to relict Mary Williamson. (Dec.
1646). Revoked on her death and administration granted to
her sister Mary Osbolston during minority of niece Sarah
Williamson. (Sept. 1657). Sh.Wi.

Willington, James, of St. Giles Cripplegate, London, who died
on ship *Burdis Factor* at Virginia. Administration to relict
Jane Willington. (Oct. 1691).

Willis, Francis, of East Greenwich, Kent, (and Ware River,
Virginia). Probate to William Willis. (Apr. 1691). Wa.

Willys, George, of Hartford, New England. Administration with
will to son George Willys during absence of relict Mary
Willys. (Feb. 1648). Sh.Wa.

Willoughby, Stephen, of Virginia. Administration to daughter
Anne Willoughby, attorney for mother Grissell Willoughby
during her absence. (July 1677).

Willoughby, Thomas, of Virginia who died at All Hallows,
Barking, London. Administration to nephew Thomas Midleton
during minority of children Thomas and Elizabeth Willoughby.
(Apr. 1657).

Wills, Bartholomew, of New England, bachelor. Administration
to principal creditor Nathaniel Yems. (Nov. 1688).

Willys - see Willis.

Wilson, Robert, of St. Mary Colechurch, London. (Brother
Richard Wilson in New England). Probate to relict Katherine
Wilson. (Jan. 1640). Wa.

Wilson, Robert, who died in Virginia, bachelor. Administration
with will to mother Katherine Jacob; no executor having
been named. (June 1651). Sm.

Wilson, Robert, of Wapping, Middlesex, who died on ship *James
and Elizabeth* at Virginia. Administration to relict
Elizabeth Wilson. (June 1699).

Wilson, Samuel, of Ledbury, Herefordshire, who died at Virginia.
Administration to principal creditor George Mason; relict
Catherine Wilson renouncing. (Apr. 1677).

Wilson, Thomas, (of Middlesex, mariner, commander of ship
   Charles; will written in Virginia), late in East Indies.
   Probate to relict Ellinor Wilson. (Jan. 1655). Sh.
Wilson, Thomas the elder, (formerly of London), late of
   Ryecroft, Rawmarsh, Yorkshire. (Cousin Thomas Brownall
   of Rhode Island). Probate to son Thomas Wilson. Feb. 1659).
   Wa.
Winch, Elizabeth, of All Hallows, London, spinster, (bound for
   Virginia). Probate to brothers Richard and John Winch.
   (May 1661). Wi.
Winchelsey, Alexander, of Limehouse, Middlesex. (Tobacco in
   Virginia). Probate to Thomas Ravenett. (May 1621). Wi.
Winslow, Edward, of London. (Bequests to poor in New England).
   Probate to son Josias Winslow. (Oct. 1655). Wa.
Winthrop, Stephen, of James Street, Westminster, Middlesex.
   (Father and mother buried in Boston, New England). Probate
   to relict Judith Winthrop and brother-in-law John Chamber-
   laine with similar powers reserved to Thomas Plampyon.
   (Aug. 1658). Wa.
Wise, John, of Virginia. Probate to mother Anne Miller. (June
   1685).
Withers, Henry, of Virginia. Administration to relict Joane
   Withers. (Aug. 1658).
Wythers, Ralph, of Cannons Episcopi, Wiltshire, who died in
   Pennsylvania. Administration to John Hall, guardian of only
   child Jason Wythers during his minority. (Apr. 1691).
Wolseley - see Mallett.
Wood, Richard, of Gloucester. (Kinswoman Sarah Barnes in New
   England). Probate to relict Mary Wood. (Feb. 1652). See
   NGSQ 61/115.
Woodbury, John, of New England who died on ship *Crowne* at sea.
   Administration with will to Daniel Berry; no executor having
   been named. (Jan. 1673). Wa.
Woodhouse, Henry, of Linhaven, Norfolk Co., Virginia. Probate
   to son Henry Woodhouse. (July 1688). Wa.Wi.
Wotton, Anne, of Calvert Co., Maryland, spinster. Administra-
   tion to mother Susanna Wotton, widow. (Mar. 1698).
Wotton, Philip, of East Budleigh, Devon. (Daughter-in-law
   Jane Bennett in New England). Probate to relict Joane
   Wotton. (Feb. 1663). Wa.
Wotton, Simon, (of Calvert Co., Maryland), who died in Jamaica.
   Probate to Thomas Wharton. (Dec. 1696).
Wotton, William, of Bristol. (Will made in Virginia), bachelor.
   Administration with will to sister Mary Meredeth; no executor
   having been named. (May 1656). Sh.Wi.
Wraxhall, William, of London, (joiner, bound to Virginia), who
   died overseas. Probate to relict Anne Wraxhall. (June 1630).
   Sh.Wi.
Wright, William, of Boston, New England, who died on H.M.S.
   Mermaid, bachelor. Administration to father Henry Wright.
   (Feb. 1695).
Wyborne, Thomas, (surgeon of New England), who died at sea,
   bachelor. Probate to Nathaniel Wickham. (Oct. 1691).
Wyett, Davey, of St. Gregory Stoke, Somerset, who died at Caro-
   lina, bachelor. Probate to brother John Wyett. (May 1685).
Wyld, Daniel, of Virginia. Probate to Margaret, wife of John
   Martin, with similar powers reserved to said John Martin.
   (Oct. 1676). Revoked on their death and administration
   granted to their only child Margaret Martin. (Testator now
   described as of Brewerton, York Co., Virginia). (Dec. 1691).
   Wa.

Wynne, Robert, of Virginia. Administration with will to Thomas
    Crane, attorney for relict Mary Wynne in Virginia. (Aug.
    1678). Wi.
Wyron, John, of Reading, Berkshire. (Daughter Grace, wife of
    William Rackstraw in Pennsylvania). Probate to Thomas Smith
    with similar powers reserved to relict Elizabeth Wyron and
    daughter Mary Moore. (May 1688).
Wythers - see Withers.

Yale, Thomas, of London, merchant, who died at Grone, Denbigh-
    shire. (Uncle Thomas Yale in New England). Administration
    with will to John Evans and Robert Harbin; no executor
    having been named. (Jan. 1698).
Yardley, Edward, of Virginia, bachelor. Administration to
    brother and principal creditor Thomas Yardley. (Nov. 1676).
Yeardley, Sir George, who died at Virginia. Administration to
    brother Ralph Yeardley during absence overseas of relict
    Temperance Yeardley. (Mar. 1629). Sh.Wa.
Yeamans, William, of St. Giles in Fields, Middlesex. (Brother
    Christopher Yeamans in New York). Probate to relict Eliza-
    beth Yeamans. (May 1687). Wa.
Yeo, Henry, of Gun Alley, Wapping, Middlesex, who died at
    Virginia. Administration to relict Hannah Yeo. (Aug. 1659).
Younge, Anthony, of St. Dunstan in East, London, who died
    overseas. (Goods in Virginia). Probate to John Gace with
    similar powers reserved to brother William Younge. (Apr.
    1636). Wi.
Young, Francis, of Stepney, Middlesex, who died at Virginia.
    Administration to relict Elizabeth Young. (July 1678).
Young, Richard, of St. Margaret Stayning, London. (Land in
    Virginia). Probate to son John Young. (Nov. 1665). Wi.

Zaines, John, of Virginia, widower. Administration to brother
    Thomas Zaines. (Sept. 1660).
Zouch, Sir John, who died at Virginia. Administration with
    will to son John Zouch; executors Sir Thomas Hutchinson
    and Gilbert Ward renouncing. (Dec. 1639). Sh.Wi.

Index of Executors, Administrators, Attorneys, etc.

Foster, Edmund 32
    John 3
    William 26
Fowlkes, Bridget 57
Frampton, Thomas 4
Fredericke, Sir John 29
Frensh, Phillip 11
Frinck, Sarah 42
    Thomas 42
Frodsham, Rebecca 56
Frost, Joanna 6
    Roger 6
Fuller, Elizabeth 14
    John 14
    Richard 49

Gace, John 66
Garland, Sarah 61
    Thomas 61
Gate, John 26
Getley, Hester 47
Gateley, Hester 47
Gay, George 56
Gelibrand, Samuel 58
    Thomas 53
Getley - see Gateley
Gibbons, Anne 5
    William 5
Gilbert, Jane 5
Gildersleeve, Isaac 40
Gill, John 56
Githins, John 30
    William 30
Glascock, John 3
Glassbrooke, William 61
Godwin, Joseph 56
Goffe, Deborah 45
Gold - see Gould
Golden - see Goulden
Gollopp, Thomas 14
Good, Margaret 23
Gordon, William 34
Gorton, Mary 38*
    Samuel 38
Gotley, Richard 46
Gould, Christopher 48
Gold, James 14
Gould, James 14
    Mary 48
Gold, Rowland 33
Golden, George 60
Goulding, Christopher 19
Graby, Richard 30
Grant, John 29
Graves, Mary 48
    Robert 50
Gray, John 13
    Sibill 52
    William 47
Greene, Francis 50
    John 1
    Nicholas 29
Greendon, Sarah 27
Gregge, Ralph 62
Gregory, Charles 21
    Oliver 30
    Susanna 21
    Thomas 50
Grice, John 58
Griffith, Thomas 36
Grove, Thomas 55
Grover, Thomas 57

Gutridge, Alice 62
Guye, Thomas 19

Haige, Obediah 36
Haisman, Ellen 59
    Henry 59
Haistwell, Thomas 57
Hall, John 43,64,65
    Winifred 19
Hallam, George 19
Hally, William 45
Hamby, Richard 17
Hanes - see Haynes
Harbin, Robert 66
Harbison, Elizabeth 5
    Susan 5
Hardcastle, William 31
Hardmett, Richard 64
Hardey, Jonathan 25
    Joseph 25
Hardy, Samuel 40
Harford, Charles 6
Harlakenden, William 51
Harlock, Elizabeth 48
    John 48
Harmer, Timothy 1
    William 1
Harris, James 45
    John 24
    Malachi 24
    Roger 47
    Susanna 12
Harrison, Thomas 47
Hart, Stephen 40
Hartwell, Henry 57
Harvey, Richard 13
    William 13
Haslewood, Anne 4
    Cuthbert 4
    John 4
Hawkesworth, Edward 56
Hawkins, Aaron 6
    Rebecca 6
    Walter 64
Hawles, Sir John 30
Hawley, Henry 63
Hayes, Patrick 33
Hayman, Sir William 15
Hayne, Robert 55
Hanes, Richard 3
Hazard, Mary 29
Henninge, Edward 42
Henshawe, Daniel 2
Henshaw, Edward 62
Henshawe, Joshua 2
Hester, John 36
Huit, Edward 46
    Sarah 46
Heydon, John 52
Heyth, John 26
Higginson, Elizabeth 22
    John 62
    William 54
Hildersley, Mark 57
Hill, Anne 53
    Charles 63
    Edward 19,31
    John 29,61
    Mary 45,58
    William 24
Hinton, Anne 23
    Thomas 23

Hitchcock, Elianor 43
Hobart, William 48
Hobbs, Frances 11
    John 25
Hockaday, Samuel 44
Hodges, Henry 28
    Thomas 6
Holioke, Elizar 47
Holliday, Anne 27
Hoole, Edward 25
Hopbourne, Patrick 8
Hopkinson, Dorothy 2
Horder, William 58
Horsey, Stephen 20
Horsmonden, Mary 22
    Warham 22
Howard, John 13
    Margaret 13
Hubberd, Isaac 16
Hubbard, Nathaniel 63
    William 49
Hubbert, Edward 52
    William 63
Hughes, Abraham 5
Huit - see Hewitt
Hull, Edward 8,37,50
Hunt, Catherine 34
Hurd, Edward 23
Hutchinson, Sir Thomas 66

Iremonger/Ironmonger,
    Elizabeth 7,33
Ironside, Gilbert 14
Isatt, William 1
Isham, Henry 9
Ivey, Anne 3

Jackson, Edward 41
    Frances 30
    John 60
    Roger 2
Jacob, Anna 60
    Katherine 64
Jacobson, Elizabeth 60
    John 60
James, Audrey 54
    Elizabeth 50
    Gertrude 54
Jauncy, James 6,36
Jauncey, Thomas 55
Jay, Sir Thomas 50
Jeffries, John 37
Jeffreys, John 59
    Walter 59
Jefferys, William 41
Jempson, Anne 23
Jenkins, Daniel 35
    Elizabeth 35
    Henry 26
Jennings, John 27
    Martha 27
    William 30
Joffey, James 6
Johnson, Barbara 18
    John 37
    Luce 38
    Mary 5,29
    Robert 13
    Stephen 18

Johnson, Thomas 5
Jones, Ann 38
　　　Charles 46
　　　Edmund 61
　　　Edward 13
　　　Henry 60
　　　Margery 6
Jordan, John 58
　　　William 20
Joye, Robert 55
Joyce, Dorothy 15
　　　John 15

Kearle/Kerle, James 14*
Kelly, Ellis 34
Kelley, Richard 10
Kelsey, George 63
Kemble, Grace 25
　　　John 25
Kent, Richard 8
Kerby - see Kirby
Kerle - see Kearle
Kersey, Henry 2
Kerye, Daniel 40
　　　Mary 40
Keynes, John 10
Kidwell, Nicholas 54
Kiffin, William 25
Kinge, Joane 53
Kings, Richard 13
Kirby, Edward 23
Kerby, Elizabeth 25
Knewstubb, Richard 40
Knight, Hannah 59

Lake, John 47
Lambe, Thomas 39
Lambert, Roger 49
Landon, Thomas 17,49
Lane, John 32
　　　Mary 34
　　　Montague 13
Langley, John 3
Lansdale, John 39
　　　-Susan 39
Latham, Carey 34
Lawrence, John 63
Lawson, Richard 61
Lee, John 38
Lea, Thomas 45
Leeke, Ralph 37
Legge, Richard 12
Leget, William 1
Leman, Edward 37
Leslie, John 14
Lewin, John 63
Lewis, James 19*
　　　Sarah 41
Lilly, John 30
Limbry, John 10
Linch - see Lynch
Linge, Thomas 53
Linsey, Alice 37
Lewellin, Robert 28
Lloyd, Richard 33
　　　Tarphena 36
Lockey, John 36
Lofty, Thomas 3
Long, Thomas 13

Lord, Mary 53
Loton, Richard 45
Lovell, Sarah 43
Lowe, Joseph 55
Luck, Sarah 61
　　　Thomas 61
Ludgar, Elizabeth 23
　　　Peter 23
Ludington, Thomas 1
Luke, John 54
　　　Oliver 54
Lunsford, Elizabeth 34
Lyddall, George 44
Linch, Thomas 60
Lyne, Thomas 5

Machen, John 57
Macock, John 21
Major, Edward 5
　　　Thomas 8,46
Makins, Thomas 6
Mandeville, Viscount 48
Manning, Robert 44
Marker, Henry 15
Marsh, William 16
Marshall, Anthony 23
　　　Nicholas 56
　　　Philip 23
　　　Stephen 51
Marsingham, Elizabeth 15
　　　John 15
Martell, Peter 26
Martin, Alexander 22
　　　John 65
　　　Margaret 65*
　　　Phillip 12
　　　Richard 42
Mason, Adam 56
　　　Anne 44
　　　Edward 58
　　　George 64
　　　Jane 51
　　　John 44
　　　Lemuel 13
　　　Margaret 13
Matthews, John 13
Maybanke, David 54
Maynard, James 16
Mayo, Anne 19
Meares, John 46
Medlicott, Henry 59
Mellowes, Hannah 53
Melton, Anthony 52
　　　Rachael 52
Meredith, Love 60
Meredeth, Mary 65
Merricke, Giles 55
Merry, Sir Thomas 46
Mervin, Mary 14
Middleston, John 56
Midleton, Thomas 64
Myles, Anne 17
Miles, Edward 16
　　　Richard 4
Miller, Anne 65
Mills, Richard 22
Moncke, Edward 23
Moore, Mary 66
　　　Mordecai 10
　　　Thomas 53
　　　Ursula 10
Morley, John 10

Morse, Daniel 30
　　　Nicholas 30
Mortimer, John 9
Mountague, Margaret 34
Mountford, Benjamin 37
Mountfort, Rebecca 46
　　　Thomas 46
Mountjoy, Mary 42
Moye, John 63
　　　Richard 63
Moyse, Joseph 55
Munday, Edward 9
Mundy, Henry 53
Murrey, John 25
Musgrave, Peregrine 19*
Mustard, Christian 19
Myles - see Miles

Nash, Alexander 57
　　　Cicely 57
Needham, Walter 4
Nelmes, Charles 1
　　　John 1
Nelson, John 36
Nevell, John 16
Newman, Edward 32
　　　Richard 32
　　　Robert 44
Newton, Thomas 31,42
　　　William 41
Nicholas, Mary 10
Noden, Hugh 52
Noell, Edward 10
Noguier, Stephen 25
Norris, Sarah 12
　　　Tobias 15
North, Arthur 25
Norton, Francis 31
　　　Mary 31
　　　Ralph 45
Noyse, Sarah 9
Nutt, Avis 50
　　　John 50

Oldfield, Thomas 32
Orbell, James 25
Oresbie, John 28
Orie, Elizabeth 1
　　　Isabel 1
　　　Merian 1
Osbolston, Mary 64
Oxenbridge, ----- 35

Palmentier, Abraham 22
Palmer, Edward 40,61
　　　Thomas 24
Parke, Richard 13
Parker, Thomas 26
Parney, Muriel 1
Parris, Dorothy 42
　　　Samuel 42
Parrott, Susan 9
Payne, Robert 8,63
Peake, Benjamin 25
Pierce, Ester 13
Peyrs, William 49

70